GRAMMAR

OF THE

BENGALI LANGUAGE,

LITERARY AND COLLOQUIAL

GRAMMAR

OF THE

BENGALI LANGUAGE,

LITERARY AND COLLOQUIAL

BY

JOHN BEAMES

GYAN

Published by

Gyan Publishing House
5, Ansari Road
Daryaganj, New Delhi-110002
Phone: 011-47034999, 9811692060
E-mail: books@gyanbooks.com

Distribution Network
gyanbooks.com
India, USA, Canada, UK, Australia

ISBN: 978-93-6280-006-0 (HB)
First Published, 1891

2nd Impression 2024

Printed at: Gyan Press, Delhi.

GRAMMAR OF THE BENGALI LANGUAGE, LITERARY AND COLLOQUIAL

Author: JOHN BEAMES

The Oxford Oriental Series

GRAMMAR

OF THE

BENGALI LANGUAGE

BEAMES

The Oxford Oriental Series

GRAMMAR

OF THE

BENGALI LANGUAGE

LITERARY AND COLLOQUIAL

BY

JOHN BEAMES

BENGAL CIVIL SERVICE (RETIRED)
AUTHOR OF 'A COMPARATIVE GRAMMAR OF THE MODERN
ARYAN LANGUAGES OF INDIA,' ETC.

Oxford

AT THE CLARENDON PRESS.

1894

PREFACE

THE excellent grammar of the Bengali language written many years ago by SHĀMĀ CHARAN SARKĀR being now out of print, and a practical grammar appearing to be required, I have compiled the present work, based on that of Sarkār, with the assistance of BĀBU PRIYĀNĀTH BHATTĀCHĀRYYA, of Calcutta, who has, at my request, consulted several eminent Pandits on all doubtful and difficult points. I have especially aimed at making the work useful to those who desire to understand the spoken language of Bengal. The existing grammars deal almost exclusively with the literary language, which, as Bengali has during the present century been enriched by copious resuscitation of Sanskrit terms, is often unintelligible to the mass of the population. Those works do not therefore adequately prepare the European student for communication with the lower and middle classes, with whom, whether as administrator, merchant, or planter, his business principally lies. It is hoped that the present work may supply this omission, while at the same time not neglecting the refinements of the higher style.

JOHN BEAMES.

October, 1893.

CONTENTS

CHAPTER I.

THE ALPHABET.

§ 1. THE CHARACTER.

The Bengali language is written in a character allied to, but distinct from, the Devanāgarī, in which Sanskrit and some of the modern vernaculars are written. The Bengali letters are derived directly from the older character known as Kutila, which is found in inscriptions as late as the eleventh century of our era, and which in its turn is a development of the still older Gupta character, which again carries us back to the forms used in the ancient inscriptions of Asoka in the third century B.C. The gradual modifications by which the Kutila alphabet has been changed into the modern Bengali can be traced with considerable clearness in inscriptions later than the eleventh century which have been discovered in many parts of Bengal.

The order and number of the vowels and consonants are the same in Bengali as in the other Aryan languages of India.

Vowels.

অ a	আ ā		
ই i	ঈ ī	এ e	ঐ ai
উ u	ঊ ū	ও o	ঔ au
ঋ ṛi	ৠ ṛī		
ঌ lṛi	ৡ lṛī		
অং aṇg	অঃ aḥ		

Consonants.

ক ka	খ kha	গ ga	ঘ gha	ঙ ṅga (gnua).	*Gutturals.*
চ cha	ছ chha	জ ja	ঝ jha	ঞ ñja (gnia).	*Palatals.*
ট ṭa	ঠ ṭha	ড ḍa	ঢ ḍha	ণ ṇa.	*Cerebrals.*
ত ta	থ tha	দ da	ধ dha	ন na.	*Dentals.*
প pa	ফ pha	ব ba	ভ bha	ম ma.	*Labials.*
য ya	র ra	ল la	ব va.		*Semivowels.*
শ śa	ষ sha	স sa	হ ha.		*Sibilants.*

Although for the sake of completeness the vowel signs ৠ ṛī, ঌ lṛi, and ৡ lṛī are included in the list of characters, they are not used at all in ordinary Bengali. They are, however, required in transcribing Sanskrit grammatical works into the Bengali character, and in Sanskrit grammars written for the use of Bengali students.

The forms of the vowels given above are the initials, and are used only at the beginning of a word; when subjoined to a consonant they take the following forms:

a (not expressed)		ā া	
i ি	ī ী	e ে	ai ৈ
u ু	ū ূ	o ো	au ৌ
ṛi ৃ			

Thus ক ka, খা khā, গি gi, ঘী ghī, চু chu, ছূ chhū, জৃ jṛi, ঝে jhe, টৈ ṭai, ঠো ṭho, ডৌ ḍau.

In the following cases the combination of consonant and vowel gives rise to peculiar forms:

র *r* with ু *u* is written রু.	গ *g* with ু *u* is written গু.
র *r* „ ূ *ū* „ রূ.	শ *ś* „ ু *u* „ শু.
হ *h* „ ু *u* „ হু.	প *p* „ ু *u* „ পু (occasionally).

When one consonant follows another with no vowel between, the two are, as in Devanāgarī, combined into one compound letter. In most cases the elements of the compound are easily distinguishable, as in স্ব sva, ক্ল kla, ম্ন mna; but there are some in which the elements are so altered as to be with difficulty recognised. The most commonly met with are the following:—

1. Nasals preceding other consonants (called in Bengali *Áṅka-phalā*):

ঙ্	*ṅ*	with	ক *ka*	makes	ঙ্ক ṅka.	ন্	*n*	with	থ *tha*	makes	ন্থ ntha.
ঙ্	*ṅ*	„	গ *ga*	„	ঙ্গ ṅga.	ন্	*n*	„	ধ *dha*	„	ন্ধ ndha.
ঞ্	*ń*	„	চ *cha*	„	ঞ্চ ńcha.	ম্	*m*	„	প *pa*	„	ম্প mpa.
ণ্	*ṇ*	„	ড *ḍa*	„	ণ্ড ṇḍa.	ম্	*m*	„	ম *ma*	„	ম্ম mma.

2. Sibilants preceding other consonants (called *Áska-phalā*):

স্	*s*	with	থ *tha*	makes	স্থ stha.
ষ্	*sh*	„	ট *ṭa*	„	ষ্ট shṭa.
ষ্	*sh*	„	ণ *ṇa*	„	ষ্ণ shṇa.

3. Miscellaneous:

ট্	*ṭ*	with	ট *ṭa*	makes	ট্ট ṭṭa.
ত্	*t*	„	ত *ta*	„	ত্ত tta.
ত্	*t*	„	থ *tha*	„	ত্থ ttha.
দ্	*d*	„	ধ *dha*	„	দ্ধ ddha.
ক্	*k*	„	ত *ta*	„	ক্ত kta.
জ্	*j*	„	ঞ *ńa*	„	জ্ঞ jńa (pronounced gya).
গ্	*g*	„	ধ *dha*	„	গ্ধ gdha.
ব্	*b*	„	ধ *dha*	„	ব্ধ bdha.
হ্	*h*	„	ন *na*	„	হ্ন hna.
হ্	*h*	„	ম *ma*	„	হ্ম hma.
ক্	*k*	„	ষ *sha*	„	ক্ষ ksha (pronounced khya).

The letter য ya when joined to a previous consonant takes the form ্য or ্য, as ক্য or ক্য kya.

The letter র ra when joined to a following consonant takes the form ´, as অর্ক arka, কর্ম্ম karmma.

When joined to a preceding consonant it is written ্র, as স্র sra. The following forms are peculiar:

ক্র kra, ত্র tra, ত্ত্র ttra, ন্ত্র ntra, ন্দ্র ndra, স্ত্র stra.

Some compound consonants followed by the vowels উ *u* and ঊ *ū* take slightly altered forms:

ভ্রু bhru, শ্রু shru, দ্রু dru, দ্রূ drū, ন্তু ntu, স্তু stu.

As in Sanskrit, the short vowel অ when it follows a consonant is not expressed, but is held to be inherent in every consonant unless its absence is specially indicated; for instance, ক is *ka*, not *k*. When the absence of অ has to be noted the mark ্ (called in Bengali *hasanta*) is used; thus, ক্ *k*, as shown in the above list of compound consonants. ত with *hasanta* is expressed by the character ৎ, as in তাবৎ tābot, চমৎকার্ chomotkār.

The sign ँ, called *chandrabindu* (i.e. moon and drop), indicates that a nasal sound is to be given to the vowel over which it stands, as চাঁদ chānd, পাঁচ pānch.

৺ to be distinguished from the preceding, is called *īshwara* (or deity), and is placed before the name of a person to indicate that he is dead, as ৺রামচন্দ্র 'the late Rāmachandra,' or 'Rāmachandra deceased.'

The characters for the numerals are these—

১	২	৩	৪	৫	৬	৭	৮	৯	০
1	2	3	4	5	6	7	8	9	0

The leading feature in Indian arithmetic being the division by four, the signs for fractions are adapted thereto. The rupee is divided into $4 \times 4 = 16$ parts, called āna, which are thus designated (units of all kinds are also thus divided):

1 āna or $\frac{1}{16}$	৴	5 anas	৷৴	9 anas	৷৷৴	13 anas	৷৷৷৴
2 anas	৵	6 anas	৷৵	10 anas	৷৷৵	14 anas	৷৷৷৵
3 anas	৶	7 anas	৷৶	11 anas	৷৷৶	15 anas	৷৷৷৶
4 anas or $\frac{1}{4}$	৷০	8 anas or $\frac{1}{2}$	৷৷০	12 anas or $\frac{3}{4}$	৷৷৷০		

When a word is repeated, as frequently happens in Bengali, it is customary to write it only once and to put a numeral after it to show how many times it is to be uttered. Thus for যে যে is written যে ২, for পুনঃ পুনঃ is written পুনঃ ২, for শ্রী শ্রী শ্রী is written শ্রী ৩. The word শ্রী meaning 'prosperity' is prefixed to names of persons as a mark of respect, and has in modern times come to be used without any particular meaning in signatures. Thus a man whose name is Rāma Chandra signs himself Srī Rāma Chandra. In other cases it is repeated as much as five times, written শ্রী ৫, before names of deities, kings, and spiritual preceptors.

§ 2. PRONUNCIATION.

A. Vowels.

অ is pronounced in Sanskrit and in nearly all the modern Indian languages as a short dull sound similar to the *u* in English *sun*, *but*, or to the *a* in *woman*. In Bengali, however, it has a sound very nearly the same as the short *o* in English *not*, *rock*, *top*. Thus অনল ŏnŏl, কথন kŏthŏn. In some words the sound is softer and longer than the *o* of *not*, thus in বন *bŏn* the *o* is pronounced so that the word sounds almost like English *bone*. The exact pronunciation of such words is very difficult to learn, and can only be acquired by listening to native speakers. For practical purposes the short *o* of *not* may be generally adopted.

As a general rule the অ is silent at the end of a word except in poetry. Strictly speaking this should be indicated by using *hasanta*, but this mark is never used except in a few Sanskrit words, or in marking some unusual pronunciation. Thus জন is *jon*, not *jono*; so also কাণ kāṇ, বাঘ bāgh, পীঠ pīṭh, ঘাট ghāṭ. অ is also silent at the end of a syllable, as in কলশী kalśī, ঘটকী ghaṭkī.

It is pronounced very lightly at the end of words terminating in compound consonants, as শব্দ śŏbdŏ, ভদ্র bhŏdrŏ, ভগ্ন bhŏgnŏ;

also in words where *anuswāra* ং or *visarga* ঃ precede a consonant, as বংশ bŏngshŏ, দুঃখ duḥkhŏ. Such words are pure Sanskrit, and in them the vowel partakes more of the short *a* sound than the *ŏ*.

It is pronounced in adjectives, as ভাল bhālŏ, ছোট chhōṭŏ, বড় bŏṛŏ. The final vowel in these cases is all that is left of the Prakrit termination in long *ō*.

So also in some parts of the verb; as in the imperative কর kŏrŏ, চল chŏlŏ; (here also it represents an earlier long *ō*); the preterite ধরিল dhŏrilŏ, the future করিব kŏribŏ, the conditional করিত kŏritŏ, যাইত jāitŏ.

Also in past participles borrowed from Sanskrit, as কৃত kṛitŏ, ধৃত dhṛitŏ; and as a general rule in all Sanskrit words which have not become thoroughly naturalized in Bengali.

আ is *ā* in 'father.' When followed by ই it is in some very common words softened to এ *e* in ordinary colloquial usage. Thus for খাইতে 'to eat,' পাইতে 'to find,' are heard খেতে 'khete,' পেতে 'pete.' In less common words this contraction does not take place, thus for গাইতে 'to sing' one could not say গেতে. The words in which this contraction occurs can only be learnt by practice.

ই is *i* in 'pin.'

ঈ is *ī* in 'machine.'

উ is *u* in 'put.'

ঊ is *ū* in 'brute,' 'rule.'

ঋ, which only occurs in Sanskrit words, differs in no way in pronunciation from রি *ri*.

ৠ, ঌ, and ৡ are not used.

এ is properly the long *a* in English 'lane,' 'mate,' or the 'ey' in 'they.' In a few words of very frequent occurrence it has a short harsh sound like the *a* in English 'back,' thus এক, দেখ sound something like 'ack,' 'dackho,' so গেল sounds like 'gallo' when it means 'he went,' but like 'gay-lo' when it means 'to swallow.' This harsh pronunciation is only noticeable in a few familiar words which must be learnt by practice. In the great majority of words the long open sound of 'lane,' 'mate' is heard.

ঐ is nearly the English *oy* in 'boy,' 'oyster,' but a little fuller and deeper. Thus ঐক্য is oikyŏ.

ও is the long *o* in 'lone,' 'note.'

ঔ is *ow* in 'how.' It is generally transliterated by *au*, as in German 'haus[1].'

অং is the Sanskrit *anuswāra*. Whatever may have been its sound in that language (a question much debated), in Bengali it is always and unmistakeably a strong *ng*, as অংশ *ŏngśŏ*, সুতরাং *sutrāng*.

অঃ is the Sanskrit *visarga*, and is only found in Sanskrit words. It is pronounced by the Bengalis as a short sharp aspiration, the vowel preceding it being uttered with an effort. It must be heard to be understood.

B. Consonants.

Only a few of the consonants require notice. The rest are pronounced precisely as in the other Indian languages, and are sufficiently explained by the English characters given against each.

ঙ, the nasal of the guttural class, is in modern Bengali only used in composition with other gutturals, but down to the close of the last century it is occasionally found alone in poetry. In composition it does not differ in sound from ং *anuswāra*.

ঞ, the nasal of the palatal class, like ঙ, should properly be used only in conjunction with other palatals. It is, however, found alone in the same way, and down to the same date, as ঙ.

ছ in Eastern Bengal is often sounded like *s*, thus ছয় 'six' sounds like 'soy,' মাছ 'a fish,' like 'māsŏ.' So deeply rooted is this pronunciation in the popular mind in those parts that words which should be spelt with a স are erroneously written with ছ (especially foreign words), thus মুছলমান for 'Musulmān.' This pronunciation, however, is condemned by correct speakers, and is not heard in other parts of the country.

---

[1] Many of these sounds might be better explained by reference to French, Italian, and German words, but it has been thought advisable to confine the illustrations to English as far as possible.

ড at the beginning of a word is the usual cerebral *ḍ*, a sound closely resembling the English *d*, but a little harsher. Native writers use it to represent the English *d*, thus 'deputy' is written ডেপুটী. The English *t* is also represented by the cerebral ট, as is shown in the above instance. In Bengali words it is *d* at the beginning of a word, as ডাল ḍāl. It has this sound also when compounded with other letters, as চণ্ডাল chanḍāl, the name of a low caste. When standing alone in the middle of a word it has the sound of a harsh cerebral *ṛ*, a sound which must be heard to be understood, as বড় bŏṛŏ. When it has this sound a dot or small circle is placed beneath the letter. When the nasal which forms the first element in a compound is written (as is often the case), as anuswāra, the ড is pronounced as *ṛ* and has a dot under it, thus side by side with the Sanskrit form চণ্ডাল there is also the form চাঁড়াল, pronounced chāṇṛāl.

ঢ is like ড aspirated; at the beginning of a word or in a compound it sounds *ḍh*, as ঢাল ḍhāl, দার্ঢ্য dārḍhyŏ. In the middle of a word and not compounded it sounds as a harsh *ṛh*, as সাঢ়ে sâṛhe. In this case it also has a dot under it.

য at the beginning of a word sounds as *j*, thus যাইতে jāite, যান jān; so also in Sanskrit words with a preposition, or other prefix, as নিযুক্ত ni-juktŏ, অযোগ্য a-jogyŏ. In the middle of a word it is *y*, as করিয়া kŏriyā, but when doubled the first sounds as *j*, the second as *y*, thus ন্যায্য nyājyŏ, কার্য্য kārjyŏ. In the latter example the য is doubled, according to the Sanskrit rule, because preceded by *r*. When it sounds as *y* it has a dot under it.

When ও is followed in the same word by আ, a য় is inserted, which though not pronounced has the effect of giving to the *o* a sound nearly the same as the English *w*. Thus খাওয়া sounds khā-wā, হওয়া hŏ-wā. This compound character ওয় is also used to express the و (v, w) of Persian and Arabic words, as ওয়াসিল, واصل wāṣil, তলওয়ার, تلوار talwār; and the *w* in English words, as ওয়ার্ড 'ward,' ওয়িল 'will,' রেলওয়ে 'railway.' Many Bengalis find a great difficulty in pronouncing *w*, and some never succeed in pronouncing it at all.

ব representing *b* (Sanskrit ब), and ব representing *v* (Sanskrit व) are not distinguished in Bengali. It takes a Bengali boy many years of training before he can pronounce the English *v*, and many never attain to it. Both as initial and medial ব is in Bengali always *b*, thus Sanskrit वर्ण varṇa is in Bengali বর্ণ bŏrṇŏ; Sanskrit बल bala is বল bŏl. Some Bengali writers have conceived the erroneous idea that the European *v* corresponds to their ভ *bh*, thus they transliterate সভা sŏbhā, 'an assembly,' as shovā, which is absurd.

শ and স are both pronounced *sh* (as in 'shovā' above). The same takes place with the Arabic letters س and ص, thus سَرِشتہ 'an office' is pronounced not Sarrishta, as it should be, but Sherista, exactly reversing the correct sound of the two Arabic sibilants. So also صاحب ṣāḥib, 'a gentleman,' is very commonly pronounced Shāheb.

It is also necessary to notice some peculiarities in the pronunciation of compound consonants.

ক্ষ, i.e. ক + ষ, is not pronounced *ksh* as it should be (except by some very accurate speakers in Sanskrit words), but *khy*, thus ক্ষতি not kshati, but khyati (or rather khĕti, as to which see below under য). When not initial, and when compounded with another consonant it sounds as *kkh*, thus লক্ষ্মী not Lakshmī, but Lakkhī. পক্ষী pŏkkhi, চক্ষু chŏkkhu.

জ্ঞ, i.e. জ + ঞ, is pronounced *gy*, as আজ্ঞা āgyā, or, with a slightly nasal sound, as āngyā.

ণ when the last member of a compound of which ষ is the first takes the sound of ট, as কৃষ্ণ sounds Kṛishṭo, বিষ্ণু Bishṭu.

ম when the last member of a compound is not pronounced, but the first member is pronounced with emphasis as though doubled and with a slight nasal twang; thus স্মরণ not smŏrŏṇ, but shshᵐŏrŏṇ (the little ᵐ above the line is meant to mark the nasal sound), পদ্ম not pŏdmŏ, but poddᵐŏ. This sound must be heard to be understood.

য when the last member of a compound is pronounced very

faintly as *y*, and in some cases has the effect of doubling the first member, thus যোগ্যতা sounds like jog-gyatā, বাক্য like bāk-kya.

When য is compounded with ব in the Sanskrit preposition বি, which before a vowel becomes ব্য, it sounds in ordinary conversation like bĕ or bĭ with a very short obscure ĕ or ĭ sound, thus ব্যবহার sounds bĕb'hār, ব্যক্তি bĭkti, ব্যতীত bĭtīt.

ব when the last member of a compound is silent, but doubles the preceding member; as দ্বারা ddārā, ঈশ্বর īshshŏr. This does not, however, take place in those Sanskrit words which have not been completely naturalized. The same may be said of ম and য, which in purely Sanskrit words would be pronounced in the Sanskrit manner. Thus পদ্ম, when it means the great eastern branch of the Ganges, is pronounced pŏddŏ with a slightly nasal tone floating about it; but when it means 'a lotus' it would be pronounced pŏdmŏ or more correctly padma.

After র and ম, as in পূর্ব্বে, কিম্বা (two very common words), ব is heard; thus pūrbbe, kimbā.

APPENDIX TO CHAPTER I.

1. *Sandhi or Euphonic Permutation of Letters.*

The euphonic changes known as *Sandhi* or junction belong strictly to Sanskrit grammar, and are not in any way observed in Bengali or in any other modern Indian language. In recent times, however, the scanty peasant dialect of Bengal has been elevated to the rank of a literary language by the resuscitation on a very extensive scale of Sanskrit words, and, as among the words thus imported into the language there are many compound words in the formation of which the rules of Sandhi have been followed, some knowledge of these rules is almost indispensable to a proper comprehension of Bengali works. Inasmuch, however, as Sandhi is only of use to a student of Bengali in so far as it affects the structure of compound words, the following slight sketch will be confined to that branch of the subject.

I. The Sandhi of Vowels. When a word ending in a vowel is followed by a word beginning with a vowel and the two words are compounded into one, the two vowels which thus come into contact are blended into one according to the following system.

Vowels are divided into simple, Guṇa, and Vṛiddhi.

The simple vowels are—short a, i, u.

long ā, ī, ū. Each long vowel is regarded as consisting of two short ones; thus a + a = ā, i + i = ī, u + u = ū.

The Guṇa vowels are created by prefixing *a* to *i* and *u*; this is called the first raising; thus a + i = e; a + u = o.

a + ī = e; a + ū = o.

The Vṛiddhi vowels are made by prefixing yet another *a*; this is the second raising; thus a + a + i = ai; a + a + u = au.

The vowel *a* itself has no first raising, as *a* + *a* would be only *ā*, but *ā* is considered by grammarians as the second raising of *a*.

When two simple vowels meet, they blend into their corresponding long vowel, thus

a + a = ā; as mura ari = murāri, *a name of Kṛishṇa.*

ā + ā = ā; as kshudhā ārtta = kshudhārtta, *suffering from hunger.*

a + ā = ā; as rāma āgamana = ramāgamana, *the coming of Rāma.*

ā + a = ā; as vārttā avagata = vārttāvagata, *informed of the matter.*

So also with *i* and *u*, of each of which only two examples need be given.

i + ī = ī; as giri īśa = giriśa, *mountain lord.*

ī + ī = ī; as mahī īśa = mahīśa, *lord of the earth.*

u + u = ū; as bhānu udaya = bhānūdaya, *sunrise.*

ū + u = ū; as bhū uttamā = bhūttamā, *the best land.*

When *a* or *ā* are followed by any other simple vowel, they blend into the corresponding Guṇa vowel, thus

a + ī = e; as parama īśvara = parameśvara, *the supreme Lord.*

a + u = o; as dāma udara = dāmodara, *a name of Kṛishṇa* ('rope-belly,' from a legend).

If followed by a Guṇa or Vṛiddhi vowel *a* and *ā* blend with it into the corresponding Vṛiddhi vowel, thus

a + e = ai; as brahma eka = brahmaika, *the sole Brahm.*

a + o = au; as kṛishṇa ojas = kṛishṇaujas, *the rigour of Kṛishṇa.*

If a simple vowel, except *a* and *ā*, is followed by a dissimilar vowel it is hardened into its corresponding semivowel, viz. *i* to *y*, and *u* to *v*, thus

i + a = ya; as ati anta = atyanta, *excessive.*

ū + ā = vā; as badhū ānana = badhvānana, *woman-faced.*

Lastly, if *e* and *o* are followed by any vowel except *a* they change to *ay* and *av* respectively, thus

e + i = ayi; as sakhe iha = sakhayiha, *friend, here!*

o + u = avu; as śambho uttama = sambhavuttama, *O Sambhu, best!*

Similarly *ai* and *au* are changed to *āy* and *āv* respectively.

II. The Sandhi of Consonants. Consonants are divided: (1) according to the organs of speech by which they are uttered, as gutturals, palatals, etc.; (2) according to their quality, as surds, sonants, etc. In the alphabet given on page 2, the first two columns of consonants are surds, unaspirated and aspirated; the next two columns are sonants, unaspirated and aspirated. The sibilants are surds, the vowels, semivowels, and *h* are sonants. In the *Sandhi* of consonants, changes of two kinds take place: (1) change of organ; (2) change of quality.

Change of organ takes place only in the case of dentals at the end of a word followed by a word beginning with a palatal or cerebral. The dentals are assimilated to the following palatal or cerebral, thus

t + ch = chch; tat cha = tachcha, *and that.*

t + j = jj; tat jāyate = tajjāyate, *that is born.*

t + ṭ = ṭṭ; tat ṭikā = taṭṭikā, *a commentary on that.*

Change of quality affects all consonants. When a word ending in a surd is followed by a word beginning with a sonant, the surd is assimilated to the sonant, thus

k + g = gg; dik gaja = diggaja, *an elephant which supports one corner of the earth.*

k + ī = gī; vāk īśvara = vagīśvara, *lord of speech.*

p + d = bd; ap da = abda, *a cloud (water-giver).*

t + v = dv; tat vishaya = tadvishaya, *that affair.*

When the second word begins with a nasal, the final surd is changed into the nasal of its own organ, thus

k + m = ngm; vāk maya = vāngmaya, *wordy.*

t + n = nn; jagat nātha = jagannātha, *lord of the world.*

There are many other changes of consonants under the operation of euphonic laws in Sanskrit, but the above are the only ones that have any practical importance for the student of Bengali.

2. *Samāsa or Composition.*

The practice of compounding words is extremely common in Sanskrit, and as large quantities of such compound words have been introduced into Bengali, it is necessary to give a slight sketch of the general rules of composition. The form of the compound word is determined by Sandhi, its meaning and the order of its constituent elements by Samāsa.

Native grammarians distinguish the following six kinds of compounds:—

1. DVANDVA. Two or more words are combined into one word, and the signs of the cases of the plural are appended, thus

Nominative: ātmīya-bandhu-rā, *relations and friends*.
Genitive: jñāti[1]-kutumbŏ-der, *of caste and family*.
Accusative: mata-pitā-digke, *mother and father*.

Such a compound may be also used in the singular, as jñāti kutumbo.

When one of the elements of the compound is omitted or understood, the word is considered a dvandva, as in Durjodhanerā, *the Durjodhans*, i.e. Durjodhan and his followers.

2. KARMADHĀRAYA. An adjective and a substantive combine together into one word, thus

nila + utpala = nilotpala, *a blue lotus*.
sat + chit + ānanda = sachchidānanda, *Brahma* (*existence, thought, and joy*).

3. DVIGU. A numeral and a substantive combine into one word. The principle of the dvigu compound has been extended to words other than pure Sanskrit, such as Persian and modern Bengali, thus

chāri + rāstā = chaurāstā, *a place where four roads meet*.
tri + mŏhŏnā = temohonā, *a place where three rivers meet*[2].

Pure Sanskrit is

tri + bhuvana = tribhuvana, *the three worlds* (*heaven, earth, and hell*).

4. TATPURUSHA. Two substantives are combined together, the former being governed by the latter. This is the commonest form of compound, and is very frequent in other Aryan languages. The former element of the compound may stand for any case of the noun; thus in English landlord is lord *of* land, steam engine is engine worked *by* steam, and so on; thus

Genitive: rāja-purūsha = *king's man*.
Instrumental: hasta-kṛita = *made by hand*.
Dative: brāhmaṇa-datavya = *an offering to Brahmans*.
Ablative: pada-chyuta = *fallen from rank*.
" sāgarotthita = *raised from the sea*.
Locative: grāma-sthita = *situated in a village*.

Numerous tatpurusha compounds have been made and are daily made

---

[1] Pronounced gyāti.

[2] These two words and several others of the same kind are probably borrowed from Hindustani.

from modern and even from foreign words. The Bengali language allows itself, in this respect, as much freedom as English. Examples are kāmār-dokān, *a blacksmith's shop;* musalmān-pāra, *a hamlet inhabited by Musulmans;* biyā-pāgalā, *mad upon marriage;* faringhi-tolā, *the European quarter.*

5. AVYAYĪBHĀVA. An indeclinable particle is combined with a substantive, thus prati-din, *daily;* yathā-śakti, *according to (one's) power.* It is not much used in Bengali.

6. BAHUVRIHI. Two or more words are compounded, the last member taking an adjectival or participial sense, such as in English 'broad-bosomed,' 'deep-bowered.' Compounds of this class are formed both from Sanskrit and from modern Bengali words; thus padma-lochana, *lotus-eyed;* mahā-mati, *having great wisdom;* chandra-badana, *moon-faced.*

CHAPTER II.

THE NOUN.

§ 3. THE SUBSTANTIVE.

THE substantive has two numbers, singular and plural; but, as in the other languages of the group, there is much laxity in the use of the two numbers, the forms of the singular, especially in the nominative case, being often used for the plural, leaving the sense to be inferred from the context.

The grammarians, following the example of Sanskrit, have established eight cases, distinguished by different terminations. Of these, some are worn-down relics of the old inflectional case-endings of Prakrit, while others are what in European languages would be called prepositions. As, however, in the Indian languages they are placed after, instead of before the noun, they may be more appropriately termed postpositions. The number of these postpositions, that is, of words which may be used in that sense, being very large, the number of cases might be indefinitely multiplied by considering each postposition as forming a separate case. For the sake of simplicity, however, it will be better to adhere to the old established number of eight cases, and to explain the force and application of the various postpositions separately.

There is only one declension, the same terminations being used for all nouns. The slight modifications which occur in some cases of nouns ending in a vowel[1] are merely matters of euphony, and

---

[1] Nouns ending in short *a* (ŏ) are considered as ending in a consonant, because the final vowel is not pronounced.

do not amount to separate declensions. The terminations, which, except in the nominative, are the same for both numbers, are the following:—

	Singular.	*Plural.*
Nominative	——	এরা, রা
Accusative	কে	
Dative	কে, রে	
Instrumental	এতে, তে	
Ablative	হইতে, থেকে	
Genitive	এর, র	
Locative	এ, এতে, তে	
Vocative	——	

In nouns ending with a vowel, the initial এ of the terminations of the instrumental, genitive, and locative singulars is elided, thus pitā, 'father,' gen. pitā-r; guru, 'teacher,' gen. guru-r; strī, 'woman,' gen. strī-r. So also the nom. plur., as pitā-rā, guru-rā, strī-rā.

Although the terminations given above are the regular, normal forms, yet they cannot be used indiscriminately. Some, in fact, are in the present day hardly used at all, and others only under certain restrictions. The question of the proper terminations to be used in each instance is one of the special refinements of this language, and requires careful study.

Two considerations must always be borne in mind:—

First; that all nouns in the language are for purposes of declension divided into three classes, denoting respectively

1. Human beings (vyakti-vāchak).
2. Living beings other than human (anyaprāṇī-vāchak).
3. Inanimate objects (aprāṇī-vāchak).

Second; that some forms and terminations are appropriate to the literary or classical style, others to the colloquial or vulgar style. In respect of this second point there are many gradations which can only be learnt by practice. Some terminations are very high flown, and only used by the most Sanskritizing class of writers; others, though used in ordinary literature, are held to be too formal for conversation even among educated persons; a third class again, though not used in writing, may be employed in polite society; while a fourth class (comprising generally the older and more genuine forms) is now considered vulgar and confined to the speech of the lower orders. For convenience of classification these gradations will be described as High, Literary, Colloquial, and Vulgar respectively.

i. In the accusative and dative the termination কে is used always for human beings, it is frequently omitted in the case of other living beings, and always omitted in that of inanimate objects. Thus the accusative and dative of সন্তান 'a son' is সন্তানকে; of কুকুর 'a dog' it is either কুকুরকে or কুকুর; of গাছ 'a tree' it is always গাছ.

ii. In the dative রে is archaic and poetical only. With inanimate objects the dative takes the terminations এ and এতে of the locative.

iii. In the instrumental এতে is literary and somewhat archaic. তে can be used only with inanimate objects; as

ছুরিতে কাট Cut it with a knife.

ঔষধেতে কোন উপকার হয় না The medicine does no good (literally, by means of the medicine any help is not).

তিনি কুড়ালিতে হাত কাটিয়া ফেলিয়াছেন He cut off the hand with (i.e. by means of) an axe.

But far more commonly, both in literature and conversation, the instrumental is expressed by adding to the stem certain words indicative of agency or instrumentality. These are দ্বারা, দিয়া, কর্ত্তৃক, and করণক.

(*a*) দ্বারা (from Sansk. দ্বার 'a door') is both literary and colloquial, and may be used both with animate and inanimate objects; as

হাত দ্বারা কাজ করিতেছে He works with (his) hands.

পায় দ্বারা চালিতেছে He walks with (his) feet.

ছেলেদের দ্বারা কাজ করা হইতেছে The work is done by the pupils.

(*b*) দিয়া (participle of the verb দা 'to give') is colloquial, and is used with animate and inanimate objects; as

তিনি লোক দিয়া কাজ করাচ্ছেন He does the work by means of people (i.e. labourers etc.)[1]

তিনি ছুরি দিয়া কলম কাটিতেছেন He cuts the pen with a knife.

(*c*) কর্ত্তৃক (from Sansk. কর্ত্তৃ 'a doer,' with affix ক), high and literary; only used with human beings and after learned words in their Sanskrit form; as মনুষ্য কর্ত্তৃক গৃহ নির্ম্মিত হয় The house is constructed by man.

(*d*) করণক (from Sansk. করণ 'an instrument,' with affix ক), high and literary, used in a similar way to the preceding, but with inanimate objects only; as কুঠার করণক বৃহৎ বৃক্ষ ছিন্ন হইয়া থাকে A large tree is (usually) cut down with an axe.

In both these two last instances, the sentences are composed mainly of Sanskrit words which it would be pedantic to use in ordinary conversation.

iv. In the ablative হইতে is both literary and colloquial. Colloquially, however, and with inanimate objects থেকে is more commonly employed.

v. The locative in এতে is high and literary, and used with honorific or respectful appellations. The colloquial form is এ,

---

[1] This sentence contains the vulgar or colloquial form of the present tense. Such colloquial forms will be used in the examples given in this book to accustom the student to what he will hear constantly. The correct form in this case would be *kŏrāitechhen*.

which after words ending in *ā* is written য়, as পিতায়. The form তে is used after words ending in other vowels, as গুরুতে.

vi. The vocative is not, strictly speaking, a case, and in fact it is excluded from the list of cases by Sanskrit grammarians. It is identical in form with the nominative, and is distinguished by certain prefixes. When they can be used alone these prefixes are more correctly regarded as interjections, and will be treated of under that head. But there are some which can only be used with a noun, and these may properly be considered as prefixes of the vocative case. There are certain peculiarities in their usage which it is important to keep in mind. They are as follows:—

(*a*) ভো (Sansk.), high and literary, applied to men only; as ভো রাজন গাত্রোত্থান কর O king, arise! (literally, make a raising of (thy) limbs.)

ভো ভো or ভো ২, high, literary, and poetical, used with plural nouns for both animate and inanimate objects; as

ভো ২ ব্রাহ্মণগণ Ho Brahmans!

ভো ২ বৃক্ষগণ Ho ye trees!

(*b*) হে (Sansk.), both literary and colloquial; as হে ধনি শুন কথা O lady, hear the tale! Colloquially almost as an interjection and somewhat vulgar; as কোথায় যাচ্চ হে where are you going? eh! Here হে may be supposed to have a noun understood after it, as in হে রাম, a contemptuous way of addressing any one, 'Ho, you fellow!'

(*c*) ওহে mostly used in questioning. It is used in good colloquial style; as

ওহে তোমার নাম কি হাঁ Ho you! what is your name?

ওহে তুমি বড় দুষ্ট ত Oh you! you are very mischievous.

(*d*) ও is colloquial and used in addressing inferiors, it is never used with inanimate objects; as

ও মেয়ে তুমি কি কর্চ Ho woman! what are you doing?

ও ছেলে তুমি কি খাবে Ho boy, what will you eat?

(*e*) ওগো is a very colloquial and familiar expression, mostly with a note of kindliness or affection. It is the common expression between husbands and wives. When used in questioning, the meaningless particle গা is added to the sentence; as ওগো তুমি কে গা Hulloh you! who are you?

(*f*) অরে (Sansk.), literary and poetical, not much used colloquially. The form হা রে however is common, indicating surprise and contempt, and is used by superiors to inferiors; as হা রে কালনা তুই মাঠে যাস নই Hulloh Kālnā, aren't you going to the field? (This is very vulgar style.)

(*g*) লো and ওলো are used in addressing women; as

কি কর্‌বি লো What are you going to do, my good woman?

ওলো মেয়ে কোথায় যাস Ho woman, where are you going?

vii. The nominative plural forms এরা and রা are archaic, high, and used with honorific terms; they are rare colloquially, and can only be applied to human beings.

viii. Very often the nom. plur. is expressed by the singular, leaving the meaning to be guessed from the context, as in Hindustani; this is specially the case with inanimate objects.

Ordinarily the plural is indicated by the addition of certain words denoting number, mass, quantity, and the like. The most usual are these:—

(*a*) দিগ (from Sansk. দিশ্ 'a quarter of the compass, region, direction,' but in Bengali strangely 'a mass, quantity'), colloquial, and used in light literature, with living beings only. Even in those words which form the nom. plur. with এরা or রা the oblique cases are formed by দিগ, thus রাজারা 'kings,' gen. রাজাদিগের. It is never used in the nominative. In the genitive the full form দিগের is often contracted to দের.

(*b*) সকল (Sansk. সকল 'all'), colloquial and literary, but not used by the best writers. Applied to both animate and inanimate objects, and in very common use. Care must be taken to distinguish between its employment as an adjective, in which case it precedes the noun, as সকল বালক 'all the boys;' and as a plural suffix, when it follows the noun, as বালক সকল 'the boys.'

(*c*) গণ (Sansk. गण 'a number, assembly,' etc.), colloquial, used only with human beings; as ব্রাহ্মণগণ 'Brahmans,' বালকগণ 'children.'

(*d*) বর্গ (Sansk. वर्ग 'class, group'), literary, used with human beings; as ছাত্রবর্গ 'scholars,' কুটুম্ববর্গ 'families,' নমস্থবর্গ 'reverend men.'

(*e*) সমুদয় (Sansk. समुदय 'heap, collection'), literary, with inanimate objects; as পুস্তকসমুদয় 'books,' রত্নসমুদয় 'jewels.'

(*f*) সমূহ (Sansk. समूह 'heap, quantity'), literary, with animate and inanimate objects; as জনসমূহ 'people,' দ্রব্যসমূহ 'things.' Strictly speaking this affix and the others which are pure Sanskrit should only be used with words in their Sanskrit form; thus কামারসমূহ 'blacksmiths' is inelegant, the Sanskrit form কর্মকারসমূহ should be used.

(*g*) গুলা also গুলি and গুলিন (probably Sansk. गुलिका 'a ball'), colloquial, used for both animate and inanimate things, and being a popular word is only used with ordinary Bengali nouns, and such Sanskrit words as have become popular, not with high-flown Sanskrit words, as ছেলেগুলা 'the schoolboys,' মেয়েগুলা 'the womenfolk,' কুকুরগুলা 'dogs.' Vulgar are such phrases as মাঠগুলা 'fields, lands,' মাছগুলা 'fishes.' গুলি is rather more polite than গুলা, and গুলিন is familiar and affectionate; as ছেলেগুলিন 'nice little boys.'

(*h*) সব (probably from Sansk. सर्ब्ब 'all,' through Hindi सब), colloquial, with animals and inanimate things; as পাখিসব 'birds,' টাকাসব 'rupees.'

In the words লোকে 'people,' অনেকে 'some people,' সকলে 'all, everybody,' we have probably a survival of the old Māgadhi Prakrit nominative in *e*. This termination as a nominative plural occurs only in these three words.

To complete the peculiarites of this language in respect of nouns, it is necessary to give here certain curious little syllables and words universally employed after nouns, both singular and plural, to effect modifications of meaning. Though almost exclusively colloquial, only one or two being admitted into the literary style, they form so striking a feature of a Bengali sentence and add so much to the expressiveness and flexibility of the language as to deserve particular mention:—

(*a*) টা, added to nouns, expresses contempt, dislike, worthlessness; as

জিনসটা (or জিনীস) খেতে ভাল লাগে নাই That stuff is not nice to eat. This is very vulgar language. জিনীস is Arabic جنس, and খেতে is contracted from খাইতে 'to eat.'

ছেলেটা বড় দুষ্ট That is a good-for-nothing brat.

ঘোড়াটা পাঁকে পড়ে গেচে The wretched horse has fallen in the mud. পড়ে গেচে vulgar for পড়িয়া গিয়াছে.

(*b*) টি is the opposite of টা, and expresses admiration, liking, niceness; as

ছেলেটি বেশ সুন্দর The child is very pretty.

পাখাটি কেমন শিশ দিচে How sweetly the bird sings.

মেয়েটি দেখতে বেশ The woman is fair to see.

(*c*) টুকি 'some, a little,' used contemptuously, with inanimate objects only; as

সে শাক খেতে ভাল বাসে না কিন্তু অনেক বলবার পর এক টুকি খেল He does not care for vegetables, but after some coaxing, he ate a little, i. e. just a mouthful or two.

আমার খেতে ইচ্ছা নাই তবে এক টুকি দাও I don't care to eat, but you may give me a morsel or two.

(*d*) টুকু used contemptuously for human beings; as

এক টুকু ছেলে এর অবার তেজ দেখ না Look at the little brat, what pluck he has, eh? (এর contracted from ইহার.)

But approvingly for inanimate objects; as

গরমের সময় এক টুকু বরফ খেলে ঠাণ্ডা হওয়া যায় In the hot weather if you eat a nice lump of ice you will get cool.

তবে এক টুকু দাও ত খাই Very well, then, give me a bit that I may eat it.

এমন জিনিস এক টুকু পেলে সন্তুষ্ট হওয়া আয় If one got a nice bit of stuff like that one would be pleased.

(*e*) খান (Sansk. ক্ষণ 'a moment of time;' but in Bengali, 'a piece') generally implies a piece of anything, but is often untranslateable in English; as

এক খান কাপড় দাও ত ভাই Give me a piece of cloth, brother.

ওই খানে দুখান সোণার পাত রয়েছে Two gold vessels have been left here (literally, two pieces gold vessel).

এক খান নোট One bank-note (literally, one piece note).

(*f*) খানিক when used alone refers solely to time; as

খানিক সময় পেলে কর্‌তে পারি If I get a little time I can do it.

খানিক দেরি কর্‌তে হবে You must wait a little.

When টা is added, it applies both to time and to inanimate objects generally; as

খানিকটা জায়গা অমি কিণিচি I have bought a little piece, i.e. a little bit of land.

খানিকটা সময় পেলে আমি করে দিব If you give me a little time I will do it.

(*g*) গোছা ('cluster, bunch'), used with inanimate objects; as

এক গোছা শাকের আঁটি A bundle of vegetables.

এক গোছা কলম কিণিচি I have bought a bundle of pens.

(*h*) গুচ্চার, said to be contracted from গোটা চার 'about four.'

The following specimens of nouns fully declined will illustrate the above remarks:—

(*a*) Human beings (vyakti-vāchak).

	Singular.	*Plural.*
Nom.	সন্তান 'son'	সন্তানেরা
Acc. Dat.	সন্তানকে	সন্তান দিগকে
Instr.	সন্তান কর্ত্তৃক or দ্বারা or দিয়া	সন্তানদের দ্বারা, দিয়া etc.
Abl.	সন্তান হইতে or থেকে	সন্তানদের হইতে
Gen.	সন্তানের	সন্তান দিগের or দের
Loc.	সন্তানে, সন্তানেতে	সন্তান দিগেতে

Note—In the plural the case-endings are sometimes added to the form of the genitive singular, as সন্তানের দিগকে, সন্তানের দের, etc.

(*b*) Other living beings (anyaprāṇi-vāchak).

Nom.	কুকুর 'dog'	কুকুর সমূহ or সকল
Acc.	কুকুর কে or কুকুর	কুকুর সমূহ কে, or as nom.
Dat.	কুকুর কে	কুকুর সমূহ কে
Instr.	কুকুর দিয়া etc.	কুকুর সমূহ দিয়া etc.
	etc.	etc.

(*c*) Inanimate objects (aprāṇī-vāchak).

Nom.	গাছ 'tree'	গাছ সকল, গুলা etc.
Acc.	গাছ	id.
Dat.	গাছে	গাছ সকলে or সকলেতে
Instr.	গাছ দিয়া etc.	গাছ সকল দিয়া etc.
Abl.	গাছ হইতে or থেকে	গাছ সকল হইতে
Gen.	গাছের	গাছ সকলের
Loc.	গাছে, গাছতে	গাছ সকলে, সকলেতে

§ 4. THE ADJECTIVE.

The adjective is invariable, having no separate forms for the genders. There is, in fact, absolutely no gender in Bengali, though in recent times certain writers have sought unsuccessfully to introduce the Sanskrit genders. Such expressions as সুন্দরী স্ত্রী 'a beautiful woman' are confined to literature, and in literature even to the writings of a particular school. The adjective, moreover, is not declined, except when it is used substantively.

The comparative is expressed in Sanskrit by adding the syllable তর, as পুণ্য 'holy,' পুণ্যতর 'holier.' This form is occasionally used in the high literary style, but has not taken root in popular language. Ordinarily the following words are employed:—

(*a*) অপেক্ষা (Sansk. অপেক্ষা 'reference, comparison'), used with the genitive. This is literary, and used in polished conversation or oratory; as

আমার অপেক্ষা তার দ্বারা হবে ভাল It will be better done by him than by me.

Or with the nominative; as

রাম অপেক্ষা শ্যাম বিজ্ঞ Shyām is wiser than Rām.

(*b*) চেয়ে (shortened pronunciation of চাহিয়া, participle of চা 'to see'), with the genitive, colloquial; as

তিনি আমার চেয়ে বলবান He is stronger than I.

বাঁশের চেয়ে কঞ্চী টক্ক The bamboo twig is harder than the bamboo (a proverb, meaning 'the dependants of a great man are more oppressive than the great man himself').

(*c*) মধ্যে (Sansk.), literary and colloquial; as এই দুই টার মধ্যে এইটা ভাল Of these two this is the better.

মধ্যে also serves to denote the superlative when more than two objects or persons are compared; as বালক তিনটির মধ্যে এইটি সুন্দর Of the three boys this is the handsomest.

(*d*) হতে (shortened form of হইতে suffix of the abl.), colloquial; as একার হতে ওকার ত লিখ্‌তে শক্ত *o* is harder to write than *e*.

The superlative may be formed by adding a word meaning 'all' to any of the above; as সর্ব্বাপেক্ষা (lit.), সকলাপেক্ষা (lit. and coll.), সবাচেয়ে (coll.), সকলের চেয়ে (coll.), সকলের হতে (coll.), সবেচেয়ে (vulgar).

§ 5. THE NUMERALS.

A. Cardinals.

The cardinal numbers in this, as in all Indo-Aryan languages, are derived with very little change from Sanskrit through Prakrit. From eleven to ninety-nine they exhibit the compound form of Sanskrit and Prakrit, and have consequently to be learnt individually.

All the cardinal numbers are indeclinable.

The forms of the cardinals, which are very similar to Hindi, are as follows:—

1 এক	6 ছয়	11 এগার	16 ষোল
2 দুই	7 সাত	12 বার	17 সতের
3 তিন	8 আট	13 তের	18 আটার
4 চার, চারি	9 নয়	14 চৌদ্দ	19 ঊনিশ
5 পাঁচ	10 দশ	15 পনের	20 বিশ

Instead of বিশ for 20, কুড়ি is very commonly used colloquially.

21 একুশ	27 সাতাইশ	33 তেত্রিশ
22 বাইশ	28 আটাইশ	34 চৌত্রিশ
23 তেইশ	29 ঊনত্রিশ	35 পঁয়ত্রিশ
24 চব্বিশ	30 ত্রিশ	36 ছত্রিশ
25 পঁচিশ	31 একত্রিশ	37 সাঁইত্রিশ
26 ছাব্বিশ	32 বত্রিশ	38 আটত্রিশ

39	ঊনচল্লিশ	43	তেতাল্লিশ	47	সাতচল্লিশ
40	চল্লিশ	44	চৌয়াল্লিশ	48	আটচল্লিশ
41	একচল্লিশ	45	পঁয়তাল্লিশ	49	ঊনপঞ্চাশ
42	বেয়াল্লিশ	46	ছচল্লিশ	50	পঞ্চাশ

For 47 সাঁযতাল্লিশ and for 48 আটতাল্লিশ are also used.

51	একান্ন	61	একষট্টি	71	একাত্তর
52	বাওয়ান্ন	62	বাষট্টি	72	বাহাত্তর
53	তিপ্পান্ন	63	তেষট্টি	73	তেহাত্তর
54	চৌয়ান্ন	64	চৌষট্টি	74	চৌহাত্তর
55	পঞ্চান্ন	65	পঁযষট্টি	75	পঁচাত্তর
56	ছাপ্পান্ন	66	ছয়ষট্টি	76	ছেয়াত্তর
57	সাতান্ন	67	সাতষট্টি	77	সাতাত্তর
58	আটান্ন	68	আটষট্টি	78	আটাত্তর
59	ঊনষাট	69	ঊনসত্তর	79	ঊনআশী
60	ষাট	70	সত্তর	80	আশী

Sixty is sometimes written ষাইট and sixty-six ছেষট্টি, so also seventy-six is written ছেহাত্তর.

81	একাশী	88	আটাশী	95	পঁচানব্বই
82	বিরাশী	89	ঊননব্বই	96	ছেয়ানব্বই
83	তিরাশী	90	নব্বই	97	সাতানব্বই
84	চৌরাশী	91	একানব্বই	98	আটানব্বই
85	পঁচাশী	92	বিরানব্বই	99	নিরানব্বই
86	ছেয়াশী	93	তিরানব্বই	100	শত or শো
87	সাতাশী	94	চৌরানব্বই		

For eighty-eight the semi-Sanskrit form অষ্টাশী is often heard; and for 100, while the Sanskrit শত is in common use, শো and শয় are also used, the latter especially after the first ten numerals, as এক শো 'one hundred,' etc.

In the writings of authors of the Sanskritizing school it is not uncommon to find the numerals used in their original Sanskrit form, for which the reader is referred to the Sanskrit grammar.

For 1000 in the literary style the Sanskrit সহস্র is used, but colloquially the Persian هزار with the first vowel lengthened; হাজার is more common. Of the higher numbers, লক্ষ literary or লাক colloquial for 100,000, and কোটি literary or ক্রোর colloquial for 10,000,000 are in common use.

The fractional numbers are পোয়া, চৌঠী, and শিকি 'a quarter;' তেহাই 'a third;' আধ, অৰ্দ্ধেক 'half;' তিন পোয়া 'three quarters;' সওয়া 'a quarter more' (from Sansk. স 'with' and পাদিক 'a quarter'), as সওয়া তিন 'three and a quarter;' দেড় 'one and a half' (from Sansk. দ্ব্যর্দ্ধ, literally 'half from two'); পৌনে 'a quarter less' (from Sansk. পাদ্ 'a quarter' and ঊন 'less'), as পৌনে পাঁচ 'a quarter less than five,' i.e. 'four and three quarters;' সাড়ে (which would be more correctly written সাঢে, from Sansk. স 'with' and অৰ্দ্ধ 'half') 'a half more,' as সাড়ে চার 'four and a half.' For 'two and a half' the word আড়াই (more correctly আঢাই from Sansk. অৰ্দ্ধ 'half' and দ্বয়ং 'a couple') is used. Distributives are expressed by repeating the noun, as দশ জনকে এক ২ টাকা দেও 'give each of the ten men a rupee,' or 'give the ten men a rupee apiece.'

Numerals always require the noun to be in the singular, as তিন জন 'three persons,' পাঁচ ঘর 'five houses.' When the noun is declined the numeral remains unaltered, as সাত মনুষ্যের 'of seven men.'

B. Ordinals.

The Bengali language has no special forms for ordinals. In modern times since the development of the language, the Sanskrit ordinals have been introduced. They are used in literature and in conversation by educated persons, and under the influence of the schoolmaster are finding their way into the speech of the masses. They would hardly yet, however, be understood by the cultivating and artizan classes generally. The first ten are as follows:—

First	প্রথম	Sixth	ষষ্ঠ
Second	দ্বিতীয়	Seventh	সপ্তম
Third	তৃতীয়	Eighth	অষ্টম
Fourth	চতুর্থ	Ninth	নবম
Fifth	পঞ্চম	Tenth	দশম

From eleventh to twentieth they are the same as the cardinals. From twentieth they are formed by adding তম to the cardinal, or by eliding the final syllable, as বিংশতি 'twenty,' বিংশতিতম or বিংশ 'twentieth.'

In conversation, even among educated persons, the ordinals are often expressed by adding the suffix of the genitive singular to the cardinal, as একের 'first,' দুয়ের 'second,' তিনের 'third,' and so on; thus একের বহিটে দাও 'give me the first book' (on the shelf, etc.) This form is only used with inanimate objects.

The Hindustani ordinals pahilā 'first,' dūsrā 'second,' and tīsrā 'third' are occasionally used slightly corrupted, to suit Bengali pronunciation, as পহেলা, দোসরা, তেসরা.

Colloquially certain words are used with numerals as with substantives to indicate shades of meaning. They are as follows:—

(*a*) গোটা, like টা, has a somewhat depreciating meaning; as

গোটা পাঁচেক পয়সা দিতে পার Can you give me some four pice or so? implying that it is a trifling sum.

গোটা দশেক বাটী হইলে হবে It will suffice if there are some ten cups.

With কত 'how many,' it implies an indefinite number; as গোটা কত দুষ্ট ছেলে দ্বারা এটা হয়েছে This has been done by a few mischievous boys.

When the noun is omitted, it is more indefinite still; as গোটা কত হলেই হবে A small number will do, or just a few will suffice.

(*b*) গুটি, like টি, indicates approbation; as গুটি পাঁচেক ছেলে চমৎকার গাইলে Some five boys or so sang wonderfully well.

With কত it is indefinite; as গরীব গুটি কত পয়সা পাইলে খুশী হয় The beggar is happy with just a few pice.

(*c*) খান and খানি are used in the same way as with the noun, but খানি expresses approbation; as দুই খানি সুন্দর ছবি দেখিলাম I saw two beautiful pictures.

(*d*) থান means 'a piece,' and is used in enumerating articles; as

দুই থান মোহর Two (pieces) mohars[1].

দুই থান কাপড় Two pieces of cloth.

(*e*) গাছ, literally 'tree,' is used in speaking of long straight things; as

দাঁড় গাছ বহে ভাল The oar rows (or works) well.

তিন গাছ লাঠি Three sticks.

It will be observed, in some of the above examples, that এক is added to numerals. This is always the case when uncertainty is implied. In this position এক may be translated 'about;' as দশেক 'about ten.'

Vagueness is often indicated by putting together two numbers of very different values; as বিশ চল্লিশ, literally 'twenty-forty,' i.e. any number from twenty to forty, or a little more or less. Natives are often vague about their age. A witness will sometimes depose that his age is দশ পঁচাশ 'ten-fifty,' meaning that he is a man of middle age! So also,

দু লাক পাঁচ লাক আমার আয় নাই My income is not two-five lakhs, i.e. I am not a rich man.

তাঁহার বিশ পঁচাশ লাক আয় আছে His income is twenty-fifty lakhs, i.e. He is a very wealthy man.

---

[1] The *mohar*, or more correctly *muhr*, is a gold coin, no longer current, valued generally at sixteen rupees.

CHAPTER III.

THE PRONOUN.

§ 6. PERSONAL PRONOUNS.

THE forms of the personal pronouns are the following:—

First Person.

	Singular.	*Plural.*
Nom.	আমি 'I'	আমরা 'we'
Acc. / Dat.	আমাকে	আমাদিগকে
Instr.	আমাতে আমার দ্বারা etc. আমা কর্ত্তৃক etc.	আমাদের কর্ত্তৃক আমাদের দিয়া etc.
Abl.	আমা হইতে	আমাদের হইতে
Gen.	আমার	আমাদের or আমাদিগের
Loc.	আমায়, আমাতে	আমাদিগেতে

In the instr. sing. the postpositions কর্ত্তৃক, করণক, and দিয়া are affixed to the form আমা, while দ্বারা requires the form আমার.

In all the cases of the plural the postpositions may be affixed to আমা or আমার; thus one may say আমাদিগের or আমার-দিগের, the latter form is more common in Western Bengal.

The above form of the pronoun of the first person is that used in literature and colloquially by all correct speakers. *Ami* is, however, by origin, the plural, and has by long use been so identified with the singular, that a new plural, *āmarā*, has been created for use when it is required to bring out the sense of plurality more clearly.

The old nominative is still in use, though it is now considered vulgar, and is only heard among the lower orders, or in very familiar conversation, in addressing servants and inferiors. It too has had a new plural invented for it, so completely has all perception of *āmi* being the real plural of *mui* died out. It runs thus :—

	Singular.	*Plural.*
Nom.	মুই 'I'	মোরা
Acc. / Dat.	মোকে, মোরে	মোদের
Gen.	মোর	মোদের

No other cases are in use, and it will be observed that in the plural the form of the genitive is used for the acc. and dat. also. In the singular, too, the gen. মোর is occasionally used for the acc. and dat.

Second Person.

	Singular.	*Plural.*
Nom.	তুমি 'thou'	তোমরা 'ye'
Acc. / Dat.	তোমাকে	তোমাদিগকে
Instr.	তোমাতে তোমার দ্বারা etc. তোমা কর্তৃক etc.	তোমাদের কর্তৃক তোমাদের দিয়া etc.
Abl.	তোমা হইতে	তোমাদের হইতে
Gen.	তোমার	তোমাদের, তোমাদিগের
Loc.	তোমায়, তোমাতে	তোমাদিগেতে

Here, also, there is the old singular, now esteemed vulgar, with a modern plural fitted to it, thus

	Singular.	*Plural.*
Nom.	তুই 'thou'	তোরা
Acc. Dat.	তোকে, তোরে	তোদের
Gen.	তোর	তোদের

The remarks regarding the first person apply to the second person also.

In addressing superiors or equals in rank, and generally in the conversation of respectable persons of all classes, neither তুমি nor তুই are used. In their place is used আপনি (from Sansk. আত্মন্ 'self'), meaning literally 'self,' but used also to mean 'your honour,' 'your honourable self,' and such like, just as in Hindi *āp*. The student must be very careful always to use *āpani* when addressing gentlemen or respectable people of any class, as the use of *tumi*, except to servants, relations, or very humble people, is regarded almost as an insult.

When used to mean 'self,' i.e. 'myself, thyself, himself,' etc., *āpani* is thus declined:

	Singular.	*Plural.*
Nom.	আপনি	আপনারা
Acc. Dat.	আপনাকে	আপনাদিগকে
	etc.	etc.

But when implying 'your honour' it may take in nom. plur. the form আপনকারা, gen. sing. আপনকার, and so in the other cases.

আপনি, when used respectfully, takes the verb in the third person; as আপনি উত্তর দিবেন Your honour will give an answer.

When it is wished to express still greater respect, the word মহাশয় 'gentleman, Sir,' is used, also with the verb in the third person plural; as মহাশয় সেখানে যাইবেন কি না Will you go there or not, Sir?

Third Person.

	Singular.	*Plural.*
Nom.	তিনি 'he,' 'she'	তাঁহারা 'they'
Acc. Dat.	তাঁহাকে	তাঁহাদিগকে
Instr.	তাঁহাতে তাঁহার দ্বারা etc.	তাঁহাদের কর্ত্তৃক তাঁহাদের দিয়া etc.
Abl.	তাঁহা হইতে	তাঁহাদের হইতে
Gen.	তাঁহার	তাঁহাদের, তাঁহাদিগের
Loc.	তাঁহাতে, তাঁহায়	তাঁহাদিগেতে

The old singular, now considered vulgar, is

Nom.	সে 'he,' 'she'	তাহারা 'they'
Gen.	তাহার তার	তাদের
Acc. Dat.	তাহাকে, তাকে	
Loc.	তাতে, তাহায়, তায়	তাদের

It will be observed that the forms of the oblique cases differ only from the higher form by omission of the *chandrabindu*, or nasal sign.

'It' is expressed by সে, and its inflection তাহা, generally contracted to তা. In this sense সে is used in correct language.

There is no possessive pronoun, the genitive of the personal pronouns is used, as আমার ঘর 'my house,' তোমার নাম 'thy name.'

§ 7. OTHER PRONOUNS.

The other pronouns are strictly analogous in form and declension to the personal pronouns. The type of তিনি may be taken as a model for all; thus

1. Near demonstrative:—ইনি 'this,' inflection ইঁহা; vulgar এ. inflect. ইহা.

2. Remote demonstrative:—উনি 'that,' inflect. উঁহা; vulgar ও, inflect. উহা.

3. Relative:—যিনি 'whoever,' inflect. যাঁহা; vulgar যে, inflect. যাহা.

4. Correlative:—তিনি (given above).

5. Interrogative:—(*a*) কে 'who?' inflect. কাঁহা; vulgar কে, inflect. কাহা.

(*b*) কি 'what?' inflect. কাহা. Besides the regular form কাহা, কি has also an inflection কিসে used in certain cases only; as Acc., Dat. কিসে, Instr. কিসের দ্বারা or কি দিয়া, Loc. কিসেতে, Abl. কিসে থেকে or কি হইতে.

There is also an interrogative form কোন্ used only with nouns; as কোন্ স্থানে যাইতেছ To what place are you going?

6. Indefinite:—কেহ 'any one,' inflect. কাহা; to which is added the vowel ও very lightly pronounced; as Acc. কাহাকেও, Gen. কাহারও or কাহারো, etc. It is used both for singular and plural, if, indeed, it can be said to have a plural. কিছু 'anything.'

কোন (to be distinguished from কোন্ 'which?'), 'some, any,' is indeclinable.

The pronouns এ, ও, সে often have an ই added to them, as এই or ঐ, ওই, সেই; this conveys a certain emphasis, as 'this very one,' etc. In the genitive plural for ইঁহাদের and উঁহাদের the contractions এঁদের and ওঁদের are used colloquially by all classes.

These pronouns also take the additional syllables টা, টি, like nouns. The inflectional terminations are placed *after* these additions, as Gen. এটার; কোনটার; Loc. এটাতে, এটায়; কোনটাতে.

There are also many compound pronouns which must be learnt from practice, such as যে কেহ 'whosoever,' যে কোন *id.*, যে কিছু 'whatsoever,' যে সকল 'all who,' etc.

The adjective in Bengali being indeclinable, it follows that whenever any one of the above pronouns is used as an adjective, it becomes indeclinable. When used adjectivally the forms এ, ও, সে, and যে are used, not ইনি, উনি, তিনি, or যিনি; as

এ পণ্ডিত কোথা থাকেন Where does this Pandit live?

ও বালক কে ডাক Call that boy.

সে ফুলগুলি তুমি কোথা পাইয়াছিলে Where did you find those flowers?

সে যে কি লোক তাহা আমি বলিতে পারি না What caste he may be I cannot say.

More usually in this connexion the forms with ই added are used, as ঐ, ওই, etc.

As possessive, meaning '(my, thy, his) own,' আপনি 'self' may be used in the genitive আপনার, or in the stem form আপন; as আপন ঘর যাও Go to your own house.

In the sense of 'own' is also used নিজ, as ঐ আমার নিজের ঘর 'this is my own house;' but when used as a substantive, meaning '(my, thy, him) self,' it takes the form নিজে, as নিজে কাজ করিল 'he did the work himself.' In this sense it is declined like other pronouns, though in the singular only.

The Persian word خود 'self,' written খোদ, is also frequently used in the same way as নিজ. It is considered as respectful, and may be used in addressing superiors; as চাকর বাকরের কথায় কি হয় খোদ কি বলেন What matters the talk of servants, what do you yourself say, Sir?

আপনি, নিজে, and খোদ are sometimes for distinctness sake added to the pronoun of the person to which they refer, and are then put in the same case as the personal pronoun; as তাঁহার আপনার (or নিজের) বিষয় তিনি রক্ষা করিতে পারেন 'he can take care of his own property,' where emphasis is laid on '*own*.'

অমুক and the Arabic فلان, corrupted to ফলনা, answer to English 'so and so,' and are used where the name of the person or place referred to is omitted; as নাম অমুক, জাতি অমুক, ঘর অমুক Name, so and so; caste, such and such; residence, so and so.

In the literary style, and especially in poetry, parts of the Sanskrit personal pronouns are not infrequently used; as, for instance, the bases of the pronouns of the first and second persons, and some of the cases. The full declension of these pronouns belongs to Sanskrit grammar, but the most generally used forms are here given :

Base মৎ or অস্মদ্ 'I' or 'we' মম 'of me' মাম্ 'me' মে 'to me.'
" ত্বৎ or যুষ্মদ্ 'thou' or 'ye' তব 'of thee' ত্বাম্ 'thee' তে 'to thee.'

The forms of the base are used in composition only; as মৎপুত্র 'my son,' অস্মদ্ গৃহ 'our house.'

The pronoun of the third person (nom. sing. neut.) তৎ is also used for তিনি 'he, that,' only in composition; as তৎকালীন 'belonging to that time,' তদ্দ্বারা 'by means of that.' Other words so used are স্ব 'self,' and ভবৎ 'your honour.'

From মৎ, অস্মদ্, and the others, are formed possessive adjectives; thus

মদীয়	'mine'	ত্বদীয়	'thine'	তদীয়া	'his' or 'its.'
অস্মদীয়	'ours'	যুষ্মদীয়	'yours'	স্বীয়	'one's own.'

Occasionally also the Sanskrit word আত্মন 'self' (the origin of আপনি) is used by some writers, and is even declined; as Acc. আত্মাকে, Gen. আত্মার; but this is rare. In composition the shortened form আত্ম is found in some words of rather frequent use, such as আত্মরক্ষা 'self-preservation,' আত্মহত্যা 'suicide.' স্বয়ং (pronounced shŏyŏng) 'self,' though a pure Sanskrit word, is often used both in literature and in the higher conversational style. It is used with pronouns of all persons, and in all cases, and is indeclinable; thus

তিনি এখানে স্বয়ং আসিয়াছিলেন He came here himself.
তাঁহারা স্বয়ং সেখানে যাইবেন They will go there themselves.
তাঁহাকে স্বয়ং যাইতে হইবে They will have to go in person.

CHAPTER IV.

THE VERB.

§ 8. CONJUGATION.

THE verb is as simple as the noun. There is only one conjugation, and there are, strictly speaking, no irregular verbs, though some few verbs in the commonest every-day use are so much contracted as to have at first sight the appearance of irregularity. On examination, however, it will be found that they are perfectly regular.

The grammarians distinguish between transitive and intransitive verbs. This distinction, however, is only of importance in the construction of sentences, the conjugation being the same in both cases.

There are nine tenses in the ordinary verb, and in each tense two numbers, singular and plural, in each number three persons. As a natural result of the rejection of the old singular of the personal pronouns, the old singular of the verb has also been rejected, and like the old singular of the pronouns is considered vulgar. It is, however, given in the paradigmas below for completeness sake, as it is frequently heard among peasants and labourers [1]. The third person singular, however, is used both in polite speech and in literature.

It is usual to give the verb in dictionaries under the form of the verbal noun in *n* (or after gutturals *ṇ*). In this view there are three classes of verbs, ending respectively in অন, ওন, and আন; thus

---

[1] In adopting this course, I rely on the authority of Sarkār, as well as on the morphological facts of the case.

1st	বলন	to speak.	করণ	to do.
2nd	হওন	to be.	যাওন	to go.
3rd	গড়ান	to make.	পাকান	to cook.

The third form comprises active verbs formed from intransitives, and causal verbs. The active verb formed from an intransitive is, it will be observed, itself a kind of causal. Thus the neuter পাকন means 'to be ripe, to be cooked,' while the active পাকান 'to ripen, to cook,' means literally 'to cause to be ripe or cooked,' i.e. 'to cook.'

There is, as mentioned above, practically no difference in the conjugation of these three classes; but the ও of the second class not being a part of the root, disappears in conjugation, giving rise in one or two instances to peculiarities of spelling, which will be noticed in their proper place. The long আ of the third class, whether active or causal, is never elided, but retains its place throughout the conjugation.

In some cases the formation of a transitive from an intransitive verb, and that of a causal from a transitive, is effected, not by adding the characteristic আ to the root, but by change of the root vowel. In these cases অ becomes আ, ই becomes এ, and উ becomes ও; in the two latter instances the final আ is also added; as

পড়ন	fall, lie.	পাড়ন	throw down, fell, lay.
জ্বলন	burn, blaze.	জ্বালন	kindle, enflame.
লড়ন	stir, move.	লাড়ন	shake, remove.
লিখন	write.	লেখান	cause to write.
ফুটন	to burst (intr.).	ফোটান	to burst (tr.).

In the literary and higher styles numerous verbs are formed by adding the verb করণ 'to do' to a Sanskrit noun; as দৃষ্টি করণ 'to see,' পরিশ্রম করণ 'to labour.' In these cases the noun remains unchanged throughout all tenses, the verb alone being inflected.

Auxiliaries.

Bengali, being analytical in type, makes considerable use of auxiliary verbs in its conjugation. Some of these are defective, only having two or three tenses, while others are complete. The ordinary auxiliaries are আছে 'is,' হওন 'to be, or become,' যাওন 'to go,' করণ 'to do,' থাকন 'to remain.' আছে is defective, having only a present and an imperfect. They are thus conjugated :—

PRESENT.

Singular.		Plural.	
মুই আছি	I am.	আমরা আছি	we are.
তুই আছিস্	thou art.	তোমরা আছ	ye are.
সে আছে	he is.	তাঁহারা আছেন	they are.

IMPERFECT.

Singular.		Plural.	
মুই ছিলাম	I was (ছু, লুম)[1].	আমরা ছিলাম	we were.
তুই ছিলি	thou wast.	তোমরা ছিলে	ye were.
সে ছিল	he was.	তাঁহারা ছিলেন	they were.

The imperfect ছিলাম is shortened from আছিলাম, etc., which was used down to the end of the last century, and may be used *metri gratiâ* in poetry even at the present time.

The method of using the various persons of the singular and plural, which of them are admitted in correct language and which are considered vulgar, will be discussed under the regular verb.

The other auxiliaries being complete follow the type of the regular verb, which here follows.

Regular Verb.

ROOT কর্ 'DO' (Sanskrit কৃ).

I. INDEFINITE PRESENT OR AORIST.

I do, may do, etc.

	Singular.	Plural.
1.	করি	করি
2.	করিস্	কর
3.	করে	করেন্

[1] See p. 47, § 9, ii.

2. Definite Present.

I am doing.

	Singular.	*Plural.*
1.	করিতেছি	করিতেছি
2.	করিতেছিস্	করিতেছ
3.	করিতেছে	করিতেছেন্

3. Imperfect.

I was doing.

1.	করিতেছিলাম (ম্, লুম)[1]	করিতেছিলাম্
2.	করিতেছিলি	করিতেছিলে
3.	করিতেছিল	করিতেছিলেন

4. Indefinite Perfect.

I did.

1.	করিলাম (ম্, লুম)[1]	করিলাম
2.	করিলি	করিলে
3.	করিল (লেক)	করিলেন

5. Definite Perfect.

I have done.

1.	করিয়াছি	করিয়াছি
2.	করিয়াছিস	করিয়াছ
3.	করিয়াছে	করিয়ছেন

6. Pluperfect.

I had done.

1.	করিয়াছিলাম (ম্, লুম)[1]	করিয়াছিলাম
2.	করিয়াছিলি	করিয়াছিলে
3.	করিয়াছিল	করিয়াছিলেন

---

[1] See p. 47, § 9, ii.

7. Future.

I shall do.

	Singular.	*Plural.*
1.	করিব	করিব
2.	করিবি	করিবে
3.	করিবে (করিবেক)	করিবেন

8. Imperative.

Do thou.

1.	(করি)	(করি)
2.	কর্	কর
3.	করুক	করুন

9. Conditional (*also* Habitual).

(If) *I do,* also *I used to do.*

1.	করিতাম	করিতাম
2.	করিতিস্	করিতে
3.	করিত	করিতেন

These are the ordinary tenses of the simple regular verb. The following additional tenses may be formed by employing the auxiliary verb থাক্ 'to remain,' with the past participle of the primary verb:—

1. করিয়া থাকি I continue to do, I usually do.
2. করিয়া থাকিলাম I continued doing, I went on doing.
3. করিয়া থাকিব I shall continue to do.
4. করিয়া থাক Go on doing.
5. করিয়া থাকিতাম I used always to do.

It will be observed that some of the forms above given are very long, they are consequently much shortened in ordinary conversation, even by the educated classes. Thus

for করিতেছে is used কর্‌ছে kŏr'chche,
" করিয়াছে " করেছে kŏrechhe,

and so with the other tenses. To pronounce these words in full as 'kŏritechhe' or 'kŏriyāchhe' would be regarded as affected and ridiculous. These contractions are used in all the verbs in the language. Thus

dekh'chche, *not* dekhitechhe, 'he is seeing;'

jāchche, *not* jāitechhe, 'he is going,' etc.

The language is not rich in participles, nor is much use made of those that exist, except in composition. They are as follows:—

Present Participle	করিতে 'doing,' also used as infinitive 'to do.'
Past Participle	করিয়া 'done.'
Conjunctive Past Part.	করিলে 'having done.'
Verbal Noun	করণ 'the act of doing.'
„	করা 'doing.'
„	করিবা 'doing.'

Illustrations of the way in which these forms are used will be found below, page 47, § 9.

The passive is formed by adding the tenses of the verb যা 'to go' to the verbal noun করা. Thus (the first person only is given):

1. Indefinite Present	করা যাই
2. Definite Present	করা যাইতেছি
3. Imperfect	করা যাইতেছিলাম
4. Indefinite Perfect	করা গেলাম
5. Definite Perfect	করা গিয়াছি
6. Pluperfect	করা গিয়াছিলাম
7. Future	করা যাইবে
8. Imperative	করা যাই
9. Conditional	করা যাইতাম

It will be observed that the forms of the verb যা, given in tenses 4, 5, and 6, are different from the rest. This is, in fact, the only point in which there exists any irregularity in the Bengali verb. The past participle of যা, with which tenses 5 and 6 are compounded, is গিয়া instead of যাইয়া[1], and the indefinite perfect is গেলাম instead of যাইলাম.

[In this respect, Bengali agrees with all the modern languages of the group in retaining a form derived from the Sanskrit Passive Participle गत, Prakrit गओ or गयो.]

Another method of forming the passive, which is much used in literature, consists in adding the forms of the verb হওন to the perfect participle of Sanskrit verbs.

The following are a few of the most frequently used of these participles, with the Sanskrit verb to which they belong. For others the dictionary should be consulted.

Root.		*Participle.*	
কৃ	do.	কৃত	done.
ধৃ	hold.	ধৃত	held.
রুধ্	stop.	রুদ্ধ	stopped.
বদ্	speak.	উদিত	spoken.
ভূ	be.	ভূত	been.
গম্	go.	গত	gone.
দৃশ্	see.	দৃষ্ট	seen.
যুজ্	join.	যুক্ত	joined.
ঋ	(causal অর্পয) entrust.	অর্পিত	entrusted, handed over.
দা	give.	দত্ত	given.
স্থা	stand.	স্থিত	stood.
বচ্	say.	উক্ত	said.
পূর (পৄ)	fill.	পূর্ণ	full, filled.
ভিদ্	break.	ভিন্ন	divided, separate.

[1] In Western Bengal the form যাইয়া is used instead of গিয়া. The same takes place also sometimes in poetry.

ভ্রম্ wander. ভ্রান্ত confused, mistaken.
শুধ্ be pure. শুদ্ধ pure.

They are conjugated thus:

Indefinite Present ধৃত হই I am seized.
Indefinite Perfect ধৃত হইলাম I was seized.
Definite Perfect ধৃত হইয়াছি I have been seized.

The participle remaining unchanged throughout.

There is a very numerous class of Sanskrit verbs compounded with a preposition used in this way. Indeed, it is only by the almost unrestricted employment of such words that an originally poor language, like Bengali, is able to find tenses for the expression of the higher and more complex ideas. The same process has taken place in our own language, where Latin participles are largely used to form verbs. It is impossible, within the limits of this work, to give a list of all the Sanskrit words so employed; they will be found in the dictionary.

The causal is formed by adding *ā* to the root, thus from কর্ 'do,' causal করা. Verbs which end in *ā* in the active, take another *ā*, which is separated from the *ā* of the root by the peculiar Bengali combination ওয় = *w* (see § 2. B. page 8), thus যা 'go,' causal যাওয়া. The *ā* of the causal remains throughout all the tenses; thus

1. Indefinite Present করাই
2. Definite Present করাইতেছি
4. Indefinite Perfect করাইলাম

etc.

Although, as previously mentioned, there are no irregular verbs, yet there are one or two much used verbs which undergo so much contraction, and occasionally also vowel change, in the mouth of the people, that it may be well to give some of the tenses as a guide to the student.

হওন 'to be' (contracted from হো).

	Singular.	Plural.
1. Indefinite Present	1. হই	হই
	2. হইস	হও
	3. হয়	হন
2. Definite Present	হইতেছি	
3. Indefinite Perfect	হইলাম	
7. Future	হইব	

Colloquially this verb undergoes the following contractions:

হইতেছে is pronounced	হচ্চে	hŏchche.
হইয়াছে " "	হয়েছে	hŏyechhe.
হইল " "	হল	hŏlŏ.
হইবে " "	হবে	hŏbe.

The verb দেওন 'to give' is very much contracted, as follows:

	Singular.	Plural.
1. Indefinite Present	1. দেই or দি	দেই or দি
	2. দিস	দেও or দাও
	3. দেয়	দেন
2. Definite Present	দিতেছি (pronounced দিচ্চে)	
3. Definite Perfect	দিয়াছি	
4. Indefinite Perfect	দিলাম	
7. Future	দিব	
Infinitive	দিতে	
Past Participle	দিয়া	
Conjunctive Past Part.	দিলে	
Imperative	1. দেই or দি	1. দেই or দি
	2. দে	2. দেও or দাও
	3. দেউক or দিউক	3. দেউন or দিউন

The verb নেওন 'to take' is conjugated precisely as দেওন.

Colloquially দেই is rare, দি is generally used. In the imperative দেউক and দেউন also are rare, দিক and দিন being used.

The verb আইসন 'to come' generally omits the ই, and in some cases the স; thus

Indefinite Present

	Singular.	*Plural.*
1.	আসি	আসি
2.	আসিস্	আইস
3.	আইসে or আসে	আইসেন or আসেন

Indefinite Perfect আসিলাম or আইলাম pronounced এলাম
Conjunctive Past Part. আসিলে or আইলে pronounced এলে

Colloquially আসে and the forms which omit the ই are used.

§ 9. REMARKS ON THE VERB IN GENERAL.

i. The second person singular (as above remarked) of all the tenses is vulgar, and never heard in polite speech. Nor is the first person of the singular much used by educated persons, though, from its being identical with the first person plural, it is only from the pronoun prefixed that one can tell whether singular or plural is meant.

ii. In the first person singular of tenses 3, 4, and 6, the termination লাম is pronounced লুম in most parts of Bengal. The old termination ইয় is now archaic and poetical, and is not heard in conversation, except among the lowest classes.

iii. The third person singular of tenses 4 and 7 sometimes has the terminations লেক and বেক respectively, as করিলেক and করিবেক. These, however, are not used by correct speakers, and may perhaps be described as provincialisms.

iv. In the imperative, when a somewhat future sense is implied, that is to say, when a person is told to do a thing, not at once, but at some future time, an ই is inserted before the termination, as 2 pers. pl. করিও. This form is also used when a certain amount of deference or politeness is intended, like the termination *īye* of Hindustani (baithiye, dekhiye, etc.). Politeness is also indicated in the third person plural by using the future tense; thus করুন is an absolute command, 'let them do it,' করিবেন 'will they (please) do it.'

v. The indefinite present or aorist is a mere statement of action with only the vaguest idea of time. It thus expresses habit or custom; as

আমি প্রায় এটা করি I generally do this.

তিনি ও থানে বসেন He sits there (i.e. that is his usual seat).

তিনি প্রায় সকালে স্নান করতে যান He generally goes to bathe early in the morning[1].

vi. The definite present indicates that the action is being performed at the time of speaking; as

আমি দেখ্‌ছি তুমি যাও I am seeing (i.e. keeping watch), you may go.

বাবু খাচ্ছেন তুমি এখানে বস The Bābu is eating, you sit here (and wait).

vii. The imperfect is used in the same sense as in English; as আমি তাকে দেখ্‌ছিলুম কিন্তু সে চলে গেল I was looking at him (i.e. examining him), but he went away.

viii. The indefinite perfect indicates past time, generally, without precisely defining the moment of action; as

আমি যাই খেলুম আর সে চলে গেল I went and ate, and he went away.

তিনি টাকা নিলেন কিন্তু রসিদ দিলেন না He took the money, but did not give a receipt.

সে ধরূল আমি ও ছেড়ে দিলুম He seized it, and I let it go.

---

[1] In many of these examples the colloquial forms of verbs etc. are given to familiarise the student with their use.

সে আমাকে মারলে আমি পলাই গেলুম He beat me, and I ran away.

ix. The definite perfect expresses the completion of an action; as আমি লিখিছি আপনি পড়ুন I have written it (i.e. I have finished the writing), be pleased to read it.

The pluperfect is often used where in English we should use the indefinite perfect, as in expressing the first of several past actions; as

আমি মাচটা ধরিছিলুম কিন্তু পলাইয়া গেল I caught the fish (lit. I had caught), but it escaped. If in this sentence, instead of গেল, we write গিয়াছিল, it would indicate that something else happened after that, as that he caught the fish again.

তিনি যখন শুয়েছিলেন্ আমি নীচে গেলাম When he fell asleep (lit. had fallen asleep), I went downstairs.

সে যাবার পর আমি ঘুমিয়াছিলাম After he went away (i.e. after his going), I went to sleep (lit. I had gone to sleep), implying that something else happened after that.

x. The future is used as in English.

xi. The conditional requires যদি 'if,' যখন 'when,' or some similar word before it, and in the subjunctive clause তবে, তা হইলে 'then, in that case,' or some similar word; as তিনি যদি থলিটা দিতেন তা হইলে আমি ধরিতাম 'If he had given me the bag, then (lit. that having been) I would have held it.' This phrase তাহা হইলে, contracted to তা হলে, is of very frequent occurrence, and is pronounced so rapidly as to sound like two syllables only, *tā'le*.

Without যদি this tense indicates habit or custom; as তিনি প্রায় ফেলিতেন আমি প্রায়ই তুলিতুম He used generally to throw it away, and I used to pick it up.

xii. The correct use of the indefinite and definite perfects, and of the pluperfect, is very difficult to acquire, as it differs very much from the English use of those tenses. Whenever an action has taken place, ever so recently, it is expressed by a past tense of some sort, in contrast to the English idiom, which regards events very recently passed as present. Thus 'I understand what you say,' would be আপনি যাহা বলিলেন তাহা আমি বুঝিলাম 'I understood what you said.' The past tense is even used for a future event, when it is so near that it may almost be regarded as having taken place; thus আমাকে ধরিতে আসিতেছেন আমি চলিলুম or চল্লুম They are coming to seize me, I am off! (lit. I have gone.) No amount of examples would put these idioms clearly before the student, but they are easily acquired by practice.

xiii. On the other hand, some Bengali authors make free use of the historic present, as it is called, expressing past events by the indefinite present. This is, however, hardly yet an established practice of the language, but rather a mannerism peculiar to certain writers.

xiv. The infinitive is by origin a present participle, and retains that sense in some cases, chiefly in phrases where continuance or progressive action is implied; as

মেয়ে মানুষটা কাঁদিতে ২ বাড়ী আসিল The woman came home crying as she came (lit. weeping weeping came).

পিতার আহার করিতে ২ অসুখ হইল Father was taken ill while eating his dinner (lit. food taking taking became unwell).

But far more usual is the infinitive sense; as

শত্রুর তাঁহাকে হত্যা করিতে ভয় নাই The enemy does not fear to murder him.

দুঃখীটা কাঁদিতে ইচ্ছা করেছে The wretched man wanted to weep.

In the phrase দিন থাকিতে কার্য কর 'work while it is day,' থাকিতে is the present participle (lit. day remaining work do), but this usage is rare.

xv. The past participle in ইয়া and that in ইলে are both used as conjunctives, i.e. in the sense of 'having done.' The difference between them is, that when the subject of the past participle is the same as that of the finite verb, ইয়া is used, when different ইলে; thus

রাজা তাহাকে দেখিয়া বলিলেন আজ আমি যাইতে পারিব না

The king having seen him, said 'to-day I cannot go.' Here it is the king who both sees and speaks.

রামকে না দেখিলে আমার মনে বড় কষ্ট হয় Not having seen Rām, in my mind there is great distress. Here 'I,' understood, is the subject of 'having seen,' but কষ্ট 'distress' is the subject of the finite verb হয়.

With the conjunction ও added, the participle in *-ile* means 'even though,' 'although;' as খাইলে ও তিনি রাজী নন 'Even though he has eaten, he is not content.' The phrase ঐ জিনিস্ কলিকত্তায় দেখিলে ও দেখিতে পাওয়া যায় is idiomatic, and hardly translatable. It means 'that article or that kind of stuff may be found in Calcutta by searching' (lit. 'having seen is found to see'). This implies that the article is rare, but may be found in some shops with a good deal of searching for it. So also খোজিলে ও খোজিতে পারি 'Even having searched, I can search,' implying that he does not think he will find it, but he has no objection to hunt for it.

xvi. The three verbal nouns করা, করিবা, and করণ are not used indifferently. To indicate the act of doing, the first is employed; thus

হত্যা করা মহাপাপ The committing of murder is a great sin.

তোমার এরূপ করিয়া বলা উচিত হয় না For you to speak in this way is not proper (lit. the speaking of you).

পুণ্য কার্য্য করা মহৎ লোকের কর্ম্ম The performance of religious actions is the business of great people.

করিবা is only used in the genitive case, usually with the postposition জন্যে 'for the sake of,' or another noun; as

আত্মাহত্যা করিবার সময় তাহার জ্ঞান ছিল না At the time of (his) committing suicide he was not in his right mind.

সে যুদ্ধ করিবার উপযুক্ত নয় He is not fitted for fighting.

আমি দেখিবার জন্যে আসিলাম I came to see (lit. for the sake of seeing).

রোগীর পথ্য দেরার জন্য যেতে হবে I must go to give the patient his food.

করণ is a high Sanskrit word, and is only used in composition with other words, as বশীকরণ 'bringing into subjection;' করণার্থে 'for the sake of doing.' In the higher style, such a phrase as করণের জন্যে, instead of করিবার 'for the sake of doing,' is met with, but it can hardly be said to have become current in the language, and is not often heard in ordinary conversation, except among the learned. Even in literature it is generally used in connexion with a Sanskrit noun; as

অনুসন্ধান করণের জন্যে For the sake of making an investigation.

দোষমার্জন করণের জন্যে For the sake of exculpation.

§ 10. REMARKS ON THE DEFECTIVE AND AUXILIARY VERBS.

1. The verb থাক্ 'stop, remain,' is used both singly and as an auxiliary. When used singly, it means to stop or remain, and sometimes to do a thing at intervals. The following sentences, some of which are highly idiomatic, will illustrate its use:—

i. Singly:

তুমি এখানে থাক You stop here.

আর থেকে কায নাই There is no good stopping here (থেকে for থাকিয়া).

আমি ও খানে থাকি বটে কিন্তু কোন খপর রাখি না I do stay there it is true, but I don't notice anything (খপর corrupted from Arabic خبر 'news, information').

মাথা খাও সেখানে থেক By my head I pray you stop there! (মাথা খাও lit. 'eat my head!' an expression used by women in urgent supplication—থেক vulgar for থাক).

থেকে থেকে তুই কি বলিস What is it you keep saying every now and then? (lit. 'stopping stopping,' i.e. at intervals).

প্রাণ থাকতে আমি এটা করব না While life lasts I will not do this.

আজি এখানে থাকলুম কাল থাকিব না I have stopped here today, but I won't stop to-morrow.

তুই থাকিতে আমার নড়বার জো নাই As long as you stop here it is impossible for me to go away.

যা থাকে কপালে, আমি চলিলুম (চল্লুম) Whatever befalls I am going (lit. 'whatever remains on my forehead,' from the idea of a man's destiny being written on his forehead).

ii. As an auxiliary:

এটা দোষের বিষয় হলে ও আমি করে থাকি Although it is wrong, I keep on doing it (করে for করিয়া).

তুমি বোধ হয় মাসে ২ তাঁহার কাছে কিছু পাইয়া থাক I believe you get something from him every month.

আমি এই কার্য প্রায় করে থাক্‌তুম্ I used to do it almost always.

গত রাত্রি আমি শয়ন করিয়া থাকিলাম Last night I slept all night (in answer to a question, What were you doing last night?).

The future থাক, as an auxiliary, expresses uncertainty or probability, not habit; as

আমি এটা করিয়া থাকিব I may have done that (i. e. I daresay I did).

যদি আমি সেখানে গিয়া থাকিতাম তা হলে তার দেখা পাইতাম If I had gone there I should have met him.

আমি প্রায় সংস্কৃত পড়িয়া থাকিতাম কিন্তু এখন পড়ি না I used generally to read Sanskrit, but I do not read it now.

এই কায করিয়া থাক Go on with this work.

It may be added, that থাক is used only in the tenses of which illustrations have been given above.

2. The verb রহ্ 'to stay,' so much used in Hindustani, is not much employed in Bengali, having been almost entirely superseded by থাক্. It is used in poetry, and colloquially in a few phrases, such as

আমি রহিতে পারি না I cannot stop.

আমি এখানে রহিতে চাই I wish to stop here.

রহিতে পার You can stop.

রহিতে দিব না I will not let you stop (lit. I will not give to stop).

3. The curious word বটে, which is really a verb (from Sanskrit বর্ত্ততে 'it becomes'), is used only in the present indefinite, and is seldom found except in the third person singular. It is regularly conjugated; thus

	Singular.	*Plural.*
1.	বটি	বটি
2.	বটিস	বট
3.	বটে	বটেন

It is generally added to verbs in all tenses, with the sense of strongly confirming or emphasizing an assertion, like the English 'really,' 'indeed,' 'I assure you,' 'certainly.' Thus

আমি এটা করি বটে কিন্তু কোন উপকার পাই না I do it indeed, but I derive no benefit (from doing it).

তুমি ওটা করূচ বটে কিন্তু কোন কাযে লাগ্‌বে না You are doing that no doubt, but nothing will come of it.

আমি সেখানে গিয়াছিলাম বটে কিন্তু তার সঙ্গে দেখা হয় নাই I did indeed go there, but I did not meet with him (lit. did not see with him, or there was not a seeing with him).

এখানে ছিল বটে কিন্তু কোথায় গেল বলিতে পারি না Yes! he *was* here certainly, but I can't say where he has gone.

যাইতে পারি বটে কিন্তু কোন কায হয় কি সন্দেহ I can go if you wish it, but I doubt if anything will come of it.

এটা হইত বটে যদি আমি এটা করিতাম This would assuredly have happened if I had done so.

It is used singly, to indicate surprise or doubt, as well as strong assertion; as

বটে তুমি কি এটা করূচ What! are *you* doing this?

বটে তোমার কি এই কায What! is this *your* doing?

বটে তুমি কি সেই What! are you the man? (lit. are you he?)

সেখানে বটে Oh yes! he *is* there.

বটে হাঁ তোমার নাম কি হাঁ Oh indeed! what is your name? (this is almost untranslatable, it is used in addressing equals or inferiors, and implies a certain amount of doubt or hesitation in asking.)

আপনি কে বটেন Who are you, please?

4. হওন, when used as an auxiliary, implies necessity; as যাইতে হয় '(I, you, he, etc.) must go.' When the pronoun is expressed it is put in the dative case; as আমাকে পরিশ্রম করিতে হয় 'I must work hard' (lit. 'to me labour to do there is'). It is used throughout all the tenses, though some are more rarely used than others; thus আসিতে হইল '(I) was obliged to come;' তোমাকে বসিতে হবে 'you *must* sit (and wait).' It is used always with the infinitive of the leading verb, as will be seen from the above examples.

5. আছে, on the contrary, when used with the infinitive of another verb, implies the power to do, or the option of doing, generally with the idea involved that it will be better to do it. Thus করিতে আছে means 'you may do,' 'you can do it if you like,' 'you had better do;' as খ্রীষ্টান দিগকে বিধবা বিবাহ্ করিতে আছে 'Widow marriage is permitted (or legal) for Christians.' It is, however, not very frequently used.

ছিল, when used as an auxiliary, implies that an action was to be done, had to be done, or was necessary for the completion of some affair. করিতে ছিল (to be distinguished from করিতেছিল, the imperfect of the regular verb) implies 'it remained to be done,' 'it had to be done.' This is also of somewhat rare occurrence.

§ 11. COMPOUND VERBS.

Some verbs, of very frequent use, are added to all other verbs in the language to modify their meaning slightly, thus forming what are called frequentatives, permissives, and so forth. In this case only the latter of the two verbs is conjugated, the former remaining either in the infinitive or conjunctive participle. The following are the combinations in ordinary use:—

i. পারণ. Is added to verbs in the infinitive to indicate 'being able;' thus দেখতে পারি 'I can see;' উঠ্‌তে পারে না 'he cannot get up;' তুমি কি যাইতে পারবে 'will you be able to go?' or less literally 'can you go?' The future of this verb is often used where in English the present would be used, as in the last-quoted instance, and as in আমি কিছুই দিতে পারব না 'I cannot give (you) anything.'

ii. ফেলন. Literally 'to throw,' is used to imply doing a thing completely, or finishing a thing, or even doing anything very much; as

বালক তুমি এই বেলা খেয়ে ফেল Boy! now eat up (your dinner), meaning 'make haste and finish your meal while I am doing something else.'

হরি ভারী হাত কেটে ফেলেছে Hari has cut his hand very badly (কেটে colloquial for কাটিয়া), as though one said 'he has cut it off and thrown it away!'

iii. উঠন. Literally 'to rise,' implies also growth, completion, and is used where in English the preposition 'up' would be employed; as in

আম টা এক্ রাত্রের মধ্যেই পেকে উঠিল The mango has ripened in one night, as we might say 'ripened up;' (পেকে colloquial for পাকিয়া.)

ছেলে টা দেখিতে২ য়ে বড় হয়ে উঠিল The boy has grown up very quickly (lit. while looking at him).

লোক টা এত খাওয়া খেয়ে উঠ্‌তে পারিবেন না The people will not be able to eat up all this food.

iv. পড়ন. Literally 'to fall,' with verbs of motion, indicates suddenness, hurry, doing anything at once; as

নেমে পড় Come down (quickly)! নেমে = নামিয়া.

চিকিৎসক এক মিনিটের মধ্যে এসে (=আসিয়া) পড়িল The physician came hurrying in in a minute.

তৎখণাৎ অনেক লোক গিয়ে পড়িল Suddenly a lot of people rushed to the spot.

v. দেওন. 'To give,' used in the sense of allowing, suffering, permitting; as

ও রে ছেলে টা কে ফেলে দিস্ না Ho you! don't let the child fall (said to a servant holding a child in his arms).

তোমাকে যাইতে দিব না I will not allow you to go.

vi. যাওন. 'To go' has a peculiar meaning only with the verb চলন; thus তিনি চলিলেন merely means 'he went,' but তিনি চলিয়া গেলেন 'he went away,' i.e. out of sight.

vii. পাওন. Literally 'to find' used to mean succeeding in doing, managing to do a thing; as

তোমাকে দেখতে পাওয়া দায় হই উঠল It was a difficult matter to get sight of you (lit. the finding to see you rose up a difficulty).

আমি ওখানে গেলে খেতে পাব না If I go there I shall not succeed in earning my living (lit. I shall not find to eat).

viii. লাগন. Sometimes, as in Hindustani, means beginning to do anything; as

আমি তাকে ধরিলাম আর গুরু মহাশয় মারিতে লাগিল I seized him and the schoolmaster began to beat him.

Often, however, it has merely the sense of continuance, or simply of doing anything which spreads over some time; as

মা গায় হাত বুলুতে লাগল আর আমি ঘুমুতে লাগিলাম My mother rubbed (went on rubbing) my limbs with her hands and I slept (went on sleeping).

ix. চাই. This word, which is only used in this one form, is said to be the present tense of চা 'to wish.' It looks, however, more like a contraction of the Hindustani چاهیی, with which it agrees in meaning. It is used with the infinitive or verbal noun. The former denotes more urgency than the latter. Thus

মাছ আনিতে চাই নইলে (= না হইলে) খাওয়া হবে না You ought to bring some fish, otherwise there will be nothing to eat.

আজ তোমার আমার বাড়ী আসা চাই To-day you ought to come to my house.

CHAPTER V.

THE PARTICLES.

§ 12. ADVERBS.

Adverbs are formed either from pronouns or from nouns. The former, or pronominal adverbs, fall into a regular threefold sequence, derived from the five pronominal types, and expressing time, place, and manner. The following table contains the principal words of each type:—

Class.	*Time.*	*Place.*	*Monner.*
Near demonstrative type এ	এবে, এখন now	এখানে, এথা here	এমন in this way, thus
Far demonstrative type ও	wanting	ওখানে, ওথা there	ওমন, অমন in that way
Relative type য (যে)	যবে, যখন when	যেখানে, যথায় where	যেমন, যেন in what manner, as
Correlative type ত (সে)	তবে, তখন then	সেখানে, তথায় there	তেমন in that way, so
Interrogative type ক	কবে, কখন when?	কোথায় where?	কেমন how?

In addition to the above, which are the ordinary colloquial and literary forms, there is a great variety of other forms, which are either compounds of the pronominal type with a noun in the locative case, or Sanskrit forms brought into use in modern times. Thus

i. *Here*, এস্থানে, এস্থলে (lit. in this place); *in this way*, হেন, এরূপ, এপ্রকার, এরকম, এমনধরা.

ii. *When*, যদা, যৎকাল, যেই; *where*, যেস্থলে, যথাস্থানে; *as*, যেন, যেরূপ.

iii. *Then*, তদা, তখনকার, সেবেলা, তৎখনাৎ; *there*, তথা, তত্র; *thus*, তথা.

iv. *When?* কদা, কতক্ষণ, কিক্ষণে, কোন সময়; *where?* কুত্রাপি, কোই; *how?* কিরূপ.

v. *Why?* is expressed by কেন or কি.

vi. An ই is often added to the series of manner, thus এমনি, যেমনি, তেমনি, কেমনি; and an ও to এখন and কোথায়, thus এখনও, কোথায়ও.

vii. The series *hence, whence, thence, whence?* is expressed by adding the sign of the ablative to the series of place, omitting the final *e;* thus *hence*, এখান থেকে or হইতে; *whence*, যেখান থেকে; *thence*, সেখান থেকে; *whence?* কোথা থেকে, contracted কো থেকে.

viii. The series *hither, thither*, etc., is either expressed by the series of place, or by adding the word দিগে (lit. 'in direction'); as এদিগে 'hither,' 'in this direction;' সেদিগে 'thither;' কোন দিগে 'whither?'

Nominal adverbs are either pure Sanskrit words in the nominative, locative or ablative cases, or modern Bengali nouns used adverbially. Their number is infinite. A few of those most commonly used are here given:—

i. *Time.*

অগ্রে } আগে } before (prior to).	অহরহ daily.
	অকস্মাৎ suddenly.
অবশেষে at last.	যাবৎ so long as.
অদ্য Sansk. } to-day.	তাবৎ so long.
আজি Beng. } to-day.	দিনে by day.

দিনে ২ daily.

কাল yesterday, to-morrow.

কদাচ at any time, ever.

নিত্য constantly.

পরে afterwards.

পরশু { day before yesterday, day after to-morrow.

পুনরবার again.

রাত্রে at night.

সকালে in the morning.

সদা } always (these two are
সর্ব্বদা } often used together).

হঠাৎ suddenly.

ii. *Place.*

অগ্রে } before (in front of).
আগে }

অধঃ } down, below.
অধোতে }

অদূরে near.

অত্র here.

অন্যত্র elsewhere.

ভিতরে within (inside).

বাহিরে without (outside).

নীচে below.

দূরে far.

সম্মুখে in front of (*vulgo* সামে্ন).

সাক্ষাতে in presence of.

উপরে above.

iii. *Manner.*

অতি very.

অতিশয় very.

অত্যন্ত excessively.

কিছু a little.

বিস্তর much.

ক্রমে ২ by degrees.

অনর্থক in vain.

প্রায় almost.

দৈবাৎ accidentally.

পৃথক ২ separately.

পরস্পর mutually.

শীঘ্র quickly.

Many adverbs are formed from adjectives by adding রূপে (lit. 'in form'), as সুন্দররূপে 'beautifully,' or মতে (lit. 'according to'), as কোনমতে 'in any way.'

Under the head of adverbs may be classed the words used in the multiplication table, 'once,' 'twice,' and so on; thus

এক একে এক Once one is one.

দুই দুগুণে চার Twice two are four.

তীন ত্রিকে নয়	Three times three are nine.
চার চারে ষোল	Four times four are sixteen.
পাঁচ পাঁচে পঁচিশ	Five times five are twenty-five.
ছয় ছক ছত্রিশ	Six times six are thirty-six.
সাত সাতে ঊনচল্লিশ	Seven times seven are forty-nine.
আট আটে চৌষট্টি	Eight times eight are sixty-four.
নয় নম একাশী	Nine times nine are eighty-one.
দশ দশকা শত	Ten times ten are one hundred.

Beyond this the numeral adverb is formed regularly by adding ম, as এগারম 'eleven times,' বারম 'twelve times,' and so on.

§ 13. PREPOSITIONS.

Prepositions, properly so called, that is, particles placed *before* another word, are inseparable. There are no prepositions of this kind in modern Bengali, but the Sanskrit words which have been so freely introduced into the modern language comprise a large number of nouns in which prepositions are compounded. Although the study of these prepositions belongs more properly to the Sanskrit language, yet as words containing them are of very frequent occurrence, even in ordinary colloquial Bengali, it will be useful for the student to be acquainted with the general meaning of the commonest among them. They correspond in meaning and the method of their application to Latin prepositions, such as *cum* (con, co-), *pre*, *pro*, *sub*, *super*, *dis*, and the like, and can never be used separately.

অধি *over*, as in অধিকার 'power, possession,' অধ্যক্ষ 'a ruler, governor,' অধিগত 'acquired, attained.'

অনু *after*, as অনুকরণ 'imitation' (lit. 'making after'), অনুচর 'a follower,' অনুমতি 'permission,' অনুসন্ধান 'searching after.'

অপ *off*, implies detraction or taking away, as অপবাদ 'accusation, libel,' অপমান 'disgrace,' অপরাধ 'crime.'

অভি *towards*, as অভিপ্রায় 'design, object' (lit. 'advancing towards'), অভিমান 'pride, conceit,' অভিযোগ 'application.'

অব *down*, implies deterioration, as অবকৃষ্ট 'deteriorated, spoilt,' অবস্থা 'state, condition' (lit. 'settling down'). In অবতার 'incarnation' there is no sense of depreciation, the word literally means 'passing downwards.'

উদ্ *up* (in composition takes also the forms উৎ and উন্), as উদ্যোগ 'industry, effort,' উন্নতি 'promotion, elevation,' উৎপত্তি 'arising from, production.'

উপ *near, next to*, implies a secondary or subordinate condition, as উপপতি 'a paramour' (lit. 'a sub-husband'), উপসাগর 'a bay' (i.e. 'a sub-sea'), উপমা 'comparison.'

দুঃ *badly* (in composition takes also the forms দুর্, দুস্, দুষ্), as দুরাচার 'wicked,' দুঃসহ্য 'intolerable,' দুরবস্থা 'distress,' দুর্ভিক্ষ 'famine,' দুষ্কর 'difficult.'

নি *downwards*, has also the idea of completeness, as নিপাত 'falling, death,' নিবারণ 'prohibition,' নিষেধ 'prevention, restriction,' নিবেদন 'petition, representation.'

নিঃ *without*, in the sense of not having, being free from (in composition also নির্, নিস্, নিষ্), as নির্দোষী 'innocent, faultless,' নিশ্চিন্ত 'free from anxiety,' নিষ্কর 'free from taxes.'

পরা *back*, as পরাক্রম 'resistance, strength,' পরামর্শ 'advice, caution' (lit. 'holding back'), পরাবর্ত্তন 'returning.'

পরি *around*, conveys sometimes the sense of completeness, as পরিপূর্ণ 'quite full,' পরিবর্ত্তন 'exchange, equivalent' (lit. 'turning round'), পরিবার 'family and servants' (as it were 'surroundings'), পরিমান 'measure.'

প্র *before, forth*, as প্রকাশ 'display, appearance,' as an adjective, 'clear, visible, manifest' (lit. 'shining forth'), প্রণাম 'bowing, salutation' (lit. 'bending before'), প্রণয় 'affection.'

প্রতি *back*, *towards*, as প্রতিজ্ঞা 'promise, declaration,' প্রতিপক্ষ 'adversary,' প্রতিপালন 'maintaining, nourishing, protecting,' প্রতিবাদী 'a defendant, respondent (in law).'

বি *apart*, as বিকল 'confused,' বিক্রয় 'sale, barter,' বিখ্যাত 'celebrated,' বিচার 'decision, judgment,' বিজ্ঞাপন 'proclamation,' বিদায় 'dismissal, permission to depart,' বিপরীত 'opposed to,' বিবাদ 'dispute.'

সং *with*, *together* (takes also the forms সঙ্, সন্, and সম্), as সংযোগ 'union,' সম্পত্তি 'wealth,' সঙ্গম 'meeting,' সঞ্চয় 'collection,' সন্তুষ্ট 'pleased, satisfied,' সন্ধ্যা 'evening,' সম্বাদ 'news.'

সু *well*, as সুখ্যাতি 'good reputation,' সুপ্রাপ্য 'easily obtainable,' সুচরিত্র 'good report.'

In the modern language prepositions are replaced by postpositions, that is, they are put *after* the noun, which is in the genitive case, and are separate, not joined to the noun. The following are the principal ones:—

অগ্রে } before.	নিমিত্তে on account of.
আগে }	পরিবর্ত্তে instead of.
অনুসারে according to.	পর্য্যন্ত as far as.
অন্তরে within.	পিছে behind.
উপরে above.	প্রতি towards.
কাছে near, beside.	বাহিরে without, outside of.
কাছে২ close to, alongside of.	বিষয়ে respecting.
তলে below, under.	ভিতরে inside of.
দ্বারা by means of.	মধ্যে in the midst of, among.
জন্যে for the sake of.	সঙ্গে with.
নীচে below.	সমীপে with, together with.
নিকটে near.	সহিত with.

§ 14. CONJUNCTIONS.

Copulative conjunctions are—

আর and.
এবং and.
আর ও } also, moreover.
আরো }
এবং, ও, also, moreover.
অপিচ likewise.
কিঞ্চ likewise.
যদি if.
যদিচ if.
যদ্যপি although.
যদিস্যাৎ if so be.

তবে then, consequently.
তথাপি yet, nevertheless.
তবু even then, notwithstanding.
পুনশ্চ again.
অতএব therefore.
যেন in order that, whereby.
অর্থাৎ that is to say, i.e.
কেননা because.
সুত্রাং or সুতরাং consequently.
তত্রাপি even then.
তথা and, also.

These are the most common, but there are others of less frequent use for which the student is referred to the dictionary.

Disjunctives are—

কিন্তু but.
কিম্বা } or.
কিংবা }
অথবা or.
কি or.
বা or.
নতু } if not, otherwise.
নতুবা }

নহিলে } if not.
নৈলে }
অন্যথা otherwise.
নচেৎ but if not, perhaps not.
হয়—নহয় neither—nor.
যদি না unless.
ব্যতিরেকে except.
ভিন্ন besides.

§ 15. INTERJECTIONS.

Many of these have been given in Chapter II under the vocative. The language delights in monosyllables of all sorts, stuck in here and there with more or less indefinite meanings. It would be impossible to put on paper all the half-pronounced sounds and obscure utterances which—in the mouth of the Bengali peasant (and it might also be said, the peasant of most countries)—do duty for articulate speech.

আ, ও, এ correspond to the English Ho, Hi, Hullo! also to Oh! and Ah! So also হে, হারে, and many others.

বাপরে 'O father!' is used to express astonishment, pain, disapproval; বাঃ বাঃ or বাহ্ বাহ্, which is more Hindustani than Bengali, expresses admiration.

ইঃ, উঃ, 'pain' (may also be written ইহ্, উহ্).

আহা, উহু, ওহো, pain, also pity, 'alas! alas!'

ওমা, মারে, মাগো, 'O mother!' (like বাপরে), distress, amazement, and the like.

হায় ২ admiration, 'well done!'

শাবাস (from the Persian شاد باش 'be joyful!') or corruptly সবাস admiration, 'well done!' 'Hurrah!' also encouragement.

ছিহ্ or ছিহ ২ reproof, disgust, 'fie!' 'how nasty!' 'for shame!'

হাঁ২ or হাঁ৩ sudden warning or alarm, 'take care!'

হা, হু, ও, etc., 'yes!'

CHAPTER VI.

SYNTAX.

§ 16. THE NOMINATIVE (কর্ত্তা).

THE two principal factors in a sentence are the noun and the verb. These act and re-act on each other, causing the noun to take this or that case and the verb this or that tense and person according to the requirements of the idea to be expressed. The syntax of the Bengali language is comparatively simple, and its chief peculiarities lie in the use of the cases of the noun. It will, therefore, be convenient to divide this chapter into sections, one of which will be devoted to each case. The rules affecting the verb will be given under the case of the noun with which they are connected, and the effect of prepositions and other particles will also be noticed under their appropriate cases.

i. The nominative is the case which expresses the agent or subject of the verb. It agrees with the verb in number and person, as in other languages. When the nominative or subject is a pronoun the honorific, respectful, literary, and vulgar forms take different persons of the verb; thus

1st person:

আমি অনেক কার্য্য করি I do much work.

মুই রোজ কলিকাতা যাই I go to Calcutta daily.

অধীন নিবেদন করিতেছে Your humble servant represents.

2nd person:

তুমি আমার কথা শুন না You do not listen to my word.

তুই কিছু করিস নে কেবল বসে থাকিস You do nothing, you only sit (idle).

এখনি আপনি এখান হইতে যান Now let your honour go away from this place.

মহাশয় আমাকে অনুগ্রহ করিয়া থাকেন Your worship is always kind to me.

3rd person :

তোমাকে না দেখিয়া তিনি কত কাল থাকিবেন How long will he remain without seeing you?

সে আমার ভাইকে ঠকিয়েছে He cheated my brother.

From the above examples it will be seen that the vulgar pronouns মুই, তুই, and সে take the verb in the singular of their respective persons, the ordinary pronouns আমি, তুমি, and তিনি take the plural, the respectful or polite substitutes আপনি and মহাশয় take the third person plural, and অধীন the third person singular.

ii. When there are two or more subjects to one verb, and they are of different persons, the verb agrees with the highest, irrespective of the order in which they stand. For this purpose the first person ranks highest, then the second, and last the third; thus

তিনি তুমি ও আমি একত্র যাইব He, you, and I will go together.

তুমি আমি ও তিনি একত্র যাইব You, I, and he will go together.

In both of these cases the verb is in the first person agreeing with আমি.

আপনি ও তিনি সেখানে যাইতেছেন Your honour and he are going there.

মহাশয় ও অধীন একই জাতি আছে You, Sir, and I (your servant) are of the same caste.

সে ও তুই এখন যাইতে পারিস্ You and he can now go.

iii. Common nouns expressing living beings (see p. 16), and some expressing inanimate objects, sometimes take the termination এ when they are the subjects of an active verb; as

মানুষে মানুষ খায় না Man does not eat man.

বেদে বলে The Veda says.

This is really a relic of the nominative form in the old Magadhi Prakrit of which Bengali is a descendant, but its real origin having been forgotten it has been regarded as a locative case, with which it is identical in form. Consequently, in nouns ending in a vowel, the termination of the locative is used, though it has rightly no place in such a construction. It is, in fact, one of those cases of misapprehension of an archaic form, so common in many languages [1]. Thus we have such expressions as the following:

তাহাকে ঘোড়ায় চাট মারিয়াছে The horse has kicked him;

এখনকার বৃষ্টিতে কোন উপকার করে না The present rain does no good;

where ঘোড়ায় and বৃষ্টিতে, though really the agents of the verbs, are put in the locative case.

So also the words উভয়, সকল, and জন (the last only when preceded by a numeral) take the termination in এ; as

উভয়ে বা দুই জনে পীড়িত আছেন Both, or the two men, are ill.

যাহাতে সকলে বা দশ জনে সম্মত আছেন তাহাই কর্ত্তব্য Whatever all, or ten men, agree to, that must be done.

It would, however, be equally correct to say দশ জন without the এ.

So also অনেক takes the final এ when used in the sense of 'some people' or 'many people,' with a verb in the singular; as

অনেকে ত্যাগ করিয়াছে তুমিও ত্যাগ করিবে না কেন Many people have given it up, why will not you too give it up?

---

[1] A similar case is the use of 'riches' (from French *richesse*) and 'alms' (from pop. Lat. *alimosina*, Greek *eleemosyne*), which, though really singulars, have, owing to their forms, been mistaken for plurals, and are now commonly so used. As late as the seventeenth century we find 'alms' used as a singular, 'asked an alms' (Acts iii. 3, Authorized Version).

iv. The distinction between the plural and singular forms is not very strongly marked in Bengali, and we consequently find plural nouns with a singular verb, and singular nouns with a plural verb, not only in the colloquial, but even in the literary style. Thus, from one page of a popular work[1] the following are taken:

রাখালেরা গোরু চরাইতেছে The cowherds (pl.) pasture (sing.) the cattle.

কোন সুন্দরী মাথায় কাদা মাখিয়া মাথা ঘসিতেছেন Some fair one (sing.) having rubbed mud on her head is scrubbing (pl.) her head.

কেহ কাষ্ঠে কাপড় আছড়াইতেছেন One (sing.) is beating (pl.) clothes on a plank.

বালক বালিকারা চেঁচাইতেছে Boys and girls (pl.) are quarrelling (sing.).

Generally, it may be taken as a rule, that when respect is intended, the verb is put in the plural, even when the subject is singular, and conversely when the subject is a person of low class, or an animal, or an inanimate object, the verb is singular even when the subject is plural; thus

প্রথম দুই এক দিন নির্বিঘ্নে গেল নগেন্দ্র দেখিতে দেখিতে গেলেন The first one or two days passed without trouble, Nagendra went along looking about him.

Here দিন is in sense plural, but has a singular verb; Nagendra, on the other hand, being a gentleman of rank, requires a plural verb.

v. In this, as in all languages, the object of an active verb becomes the subject of a passive verb; thus, if we construct a sentence with an active verb, as

আজি আমি একটা চোরকে ধরিয়াছি To-day I have caught a thief,

চোরকে is in the accusative, being the object; but if we construct

---

[1] Bishabṛiksha, p. 2, by Rai Bankim Chandra Chatterjee Bahadur.

the sentence with a passive verb চোর becomes the subject, and is put in the nominative; as

আজি একটা চোর ধরা গিয়াছে To-day a thief has been caught.

In such a sentence the agent should be in the instrumental; as

আমার কর্ত্তৃক চোর ধরা গিয়াছে By me a thief has been caught.

But although in the literary style the insertion of the instrumental is permissible, it is never inserted in colloquial language. The use of the passive construction moreover, though not incorrect, is not frequent.

vi. Somewhat peculiar is the use of the impersonal or neuter construction in which the nominative is not expressed, and, in fact, is hardly even implied; thus

এ পথে চলা যায় না lit. In this road it is not gone.

এ জলে নাওয়া যায় না In this water it is not bathed.

This means, of course, 'one cannot go by this road,' 'one cannot bathe in this water,' or 'people do not go,' either because the road is impassable, or because it is unused, or for any other reason. Thé construction is called by native grammarians ভাববাচ্য Bhābabāchya, or 'expression of condition.' It merely expresses the state or condition of a thing, and is almost untranslateable in European languages. The student will, perhaps, at first find it a difficulty, but he will soon become familiar with it from frequent use.

Two other forms of the Bhābabāchya are of frequent occurrence. In the first of these the verb আছে is used with a past participle, and the agent is put in the genitive case; thus

তাঁহাকে আমার জানা আছে (lit. of me him known it is) I know him.

রঘুবংশের অধিকাংশ আমার দেখা আছে I have seen (read) the greater part of the Raghuvaṇśa.

In the second the verb হওন is used, also with a past participle, and with the agent in the genitive; as

তাহার খাওয়া হইয়াছে He has eaten.

ঘোড়াকে নীলামে পাঠান হইয়াছিল The horse had been sent to the auction.

The construction with আছে is usually employed when the verb is active, that with হওন when the verb is neuter, but this rule is not strictly observed. In the last illustration it will be observed that the agent is not mentioned, the sentence being a purely impersonal one. So also in the phrase

আপনাকে আবশ্যক মতে ডাকা যাইবে You shall be called when necessary,

there is no agent. It is not said by whom he should be called.

vii. When the reciprocal, mutual, or joint action of several agents is indicated, the subject is in the plural and the verb is singular; thus

জেলেরা ও চাষারা উভয়ে দুর্ভিক্ষে কষ্ট পাইতেছে The fishermen and peasants are both suffering from famine.

দাসদাসীরা কলহ করিতেছে The male and female servants are quarrelling with one another.

বালকেরা বলাবলি করিতেছে The boys are chattering together.

Usually, some such word as পরস্পর 'mutually,' 'with one another,' or উভয়ে 'both,' is inserted; as

তাঁহারা পরস্পর তাকাতাকি করিয়া লিখিতেছে They are looking at one another while they are writing.

Mutual or reciprocal action may, however, be expressed in other ways. Thus where it is intended to emphasize the action of one of the two parties, the chief party is expressed by the nominative, and the other by the genitive, governed by সঙ্গে, সহিত, or some similar postposition; as

তোমার পুত্র তাহার সঙ্গে মারামারি করিয়াছে Your son has had a fight with him (lit. your son with him a mutual beating has made).

Or, the action being put in the nominative, the agents may be in the locative; as

তাতে আমাতে বাগবিতণ্ডা হইয়াছে He and I have had a wordy quarrel (lit. in, or with, him and with me a wrangling there has been).

Or, the action being in the nominative, one agent may be in the genitive with সঙ্গে, and the other in the genitive alone; as

তার সঙ্গে আমার বাগবিতণ্ডা হইয়াছে He and I have had a discussion (lit. with him of me a mutual war of words there has been).

It will be observed that in all these sentences the action is expressed by a noun made up of two verbal roots joined together, such as বলাবলি, মারামারি, etc. Formations of this kind are excessively common in the colloquial language.

viii. Where two or more plural nouns are the subjects of a verb the termination of the nominative plural is added to the last of them only; as

দাস দাসীরা জলের ভার আনিতেছে Male and female servants are bringing water (lit. a load of water).

নর নারীরা স্নান করিতেছে Men and women are bathing.

§ 17. THE ACCUSATIVE (কর্ম্ম).

The accusative expresses the direct object of the active verb; as রাম শ্যামকে মারিলেন Rām beat Shyām.

i. The only point requiring special notice in regard to this case is the insertion or omission of the termination কে. In general the rule given at p. 17, par. i, holds good. With human beings it is inserted; with other living beings it is sometimes inserted, sometimes omitted; with inanimate objects it is omitted. This general rule, however, like most rules, is subject to certain conditions and restrictions. The termination কে may thus be omitted in the case of human beings in hasty or contemptuous speech; as

ব্রাহ্মণ ডাক Call a Brahman.

এ লোক না লও অন্য লোক দিব Do not take these (bad) people I will give you other (better) people.

কামার আনিয়া এই সিন্দুকটা খোলাও Call a blacksmith, and have this box opened.

When a numeral, or the word জন with a numeral prefixed, precedes the noun, the termination is omitted; as

আজি আমি এক আশ্চার্য মনুষ্য দেখিয়াছি To-day I have seen a wonderful man.

তিনি কল্য দ্বাদশ জন ব্রাহ্মণ ভোজন করাইবেন To-morrow he will feast twelve Brahmans.

When the particles টা and টি are affixed to nouns indicating human beings কে may optionally be inserted or omitted; as

কালি কয়টা মুটিয়া চাও How many bearers do you want to-morrow?

দাসীটি কে ডাকিয়া আন Call a maidservant.

Another class of sentence in which কে is omitted after human beings will be found below under the dative, § 18. i.

With regard to living beings not human, there is also a distinction. When large animals are spoken of, কে is generally used; as

সিংহ কে পশুরাজ কহে They call the lion the king of beasts.

But with small animals it is usually omitted; as

ইন্দুর ট তাড়াও Drive away the rat;

unless emphasis is intended, in which case it is inserted; as

এই ইন্দুর কে তাড়াও Drive away *this* rat.

With the affixes টা and টি the rule is the same as for human beings; as

আমি এই পাখিটি or পাখিটি কে পুষিব I will tame this bird.

ii. When the object of a verb is cognate to the verb, that is to say, is the noun of action of the verb, it does not take কে; as

আজি আচ্ছা এক ঘুম ঘুমাইয়াছি To-day I have slept a good sleep.

তিনি এমন দোড় দোড়িয়াছে He has run such a race.

Such expressions as 'to sleep a sleep,' 'to run a running,' 'to beat a beating,' are very common in Bengali, far more so than in English. In them the object of the verb is a noun from the same root as the verb itself, for which reason it is said to be cognate to the verb.

iii. When two nouns, denoting either animate or inanimate things, are the objects of the same verb, the first takes কে, the second does not; as

পরমেশ্বর দীনকে অদীন করিতে পারেন God can make the poor rich.

মনুষ্যকে ধূলি ও ধূলিকে মনুষ্য করিতে পারেন He can make man dust, and dust man (i.e. can turn man into dust, etc.).

In the first of these instances the nouns are both adjectives, the first, however, is used as a substantive, the latter is not so used, and consequently cannot take the termination. In the second instance, however, there is no such distinction, and the latter of the two nouns must be considered as an accusative without its termination.

iv. When the verb দেখান or its equivalent দেখা যাওন is used in the sense of 'to seem,' 'to appear,' 'to look,' it is regarded as Bhābabāchya (see p. 71), and the agent is placed in the accusative case. If a human being the noun takes কে, if a living thing not human it takes কে only when the affix টা or টি is used, if an inanimate object it may optionally take কে after টা or টি; as

এ ব্যক্তিকে পীড়িত দেখাইতেছে This person looks ill.

তোমাকে বিমর্ষ দেখা যাচ্চে কেন Why do you look sad?

এ গাছটা or গাছটাকে নিস্তেজ দেখাইতেছে This tree looks weak.

v. After a compound verb the object, if a living thing, always takes কে; as

সে তোমাকে বুদ্ধিমান করিয়া দিতে পারে He can make you wise.

তিনি গুরুকে ভক্তি করেন He worships his spiritual teacher.

§ 18. THE DATIVE (সম্প্রদান).

This case is used in the same way as in English; as it has the same termination কে as the accusative it is often confounded with it, indeed it might almost be treated as one case with the accusative, under the common name of 'objective.'

i. The termination কে is seldom omitted from the dative. Thus, when a verb of giving or speaking to, or a causal, has two objects, one denoting the thing given, the other the person to whom it is given, the former (accusative) does not take the termination, the latter (dative) does; as

গুরু মহাশয় আমাকে এক খানি পুস্তক দিয়াছিলেন The schoolmaster had given me a book.

রাম শ্যামকে কন্যাদান করিলেন Rām gave his daughter in marriage to Shyām (lit. Rām to Shyām maiden-gift made).

পণ্ডিত তাহাকে বেদ পড়াইলেন The Pandit taught him the Veda (lit. caused him to read the Veda).

রাজা মন্ত্রীকে এই কথা বলিলেন The king said this word to the minister.

ii. Sometimes in poetry, and in a few rare instances in colloquial speech, the dative takes the termination এরে; as রামেরে দেও 'give (it) to Rām.' With personal pronouns ending in ā, the termination becomes রে; as আমারে, তাহারে বল 'speak to me, to him.'

With the pronouns of the first and second persons this termination is sometimes shortened to এ, or after ā to য়; as

তোমায় কে বিশ্বাস করিবে Who will trust to you?

আমায় কে খেতে দিবে Who will give me to eat?

iii. Colloquially, in the plural, the genitive is substituted for the dative and accusative; as মাঝিদের ডাক 'call the boatmen,' আমাদের দেও 'give to me.'

iv. The dative is used after the word ধিক্ 'fie!' as পাপীকে ধিক 'fie on the wicked man!' তোমাকে ধিক থাক 'fie upon you!'

v. The dative is also used after the word নমস্কার 'reverence, homage;' as

নমস্থ ব্যক্তিকে নমস্কার Reverence to the reverend man!

vi. With inanimate objects the termination এ, which is the same as that of the locative, is used; as

অশ্বথ বৃক্ষে জল দেও Give water to the pipal tree (lit. *on* or *in* the tree).

§ 19. THE INSTRUMENTAL (করণ).

The person or thing by the agency of which any action is performed is expressed by the instrumental. The various terminations of this case have been given on p. 17.

i. As mentioned in par. v, under the nominative, when the verb is put in the passive voice, the agent is in the instrumental; as

রাম কর্ত্তৃক শ্যাম ধৃত হইলেন By Rām, Shyām was caught.
আমার দ্বারা এ কায হইতে পারে না By me this work cannot be done.

This construction is more frequent in the literary than in the colloquial style.

ii. The instrumental when used with causal verbs takes the double termination কে and দিয়া to indicate the person by whose means the action is caused; as

আমি এ কথা তাঁহাকে আপনি বলিতে পারিব না, কিন্তু রামকে দিয়া তাঁহাকে বলাইব I cannot tell him this myself, but I will cause it to be told to him by Rām.

This construction is more frequently used in Western Bengal. In other parts দ্বারা with the genitive is more usual; as রামের দ্বারা বলাইব. In the vulgar colloquial speech রামকে দিয়ে is used, and কে is sometimes omitted; as

জালিয়া দিয়া পুষ্করিণীর মৎস্য ধরাও Cause the fish of the tank to be caught by fishermen;

where the vulgar would say জেলে কে দিয়ে or জেলেদের দিয়ে.

iii. Although, as mentioned in p. 18, দ্বারা is used as a simple termination with the nominal stem to form the instrumental, it is also, as shown in the last example on that page (ছেলেদের দ্বারা), affixed to the genitive case in the manner of a postposition. Purists affirm that strictly speaking when the noun is pure Sanskrit দ্বারা should be used with the nominative; when it is Bengali, with the genitive. Thus, they would say অশ্বদ্বারা 'by a horse,' because অশ্ব is a pure Sanskrit word, but ঘোড়ার দ্বারা because ঘোড়া is a modern Bengali word. This distinction, like many others introduced by the Sanskritizing school, is not universally observed.

§ 20. THE ABLATIVE (অপাদান).

This case, as in other languages, indicates the person, place or thing, from which the subject is taken away, removed or obtained. There is no special peculiarity in the use of this case, the following idiomatic usages may be noted.

i. When it is desired to express the idea of receiving anything from a person some word indicating nearness, possession, or the like, is inserted; as

আমি তাঁহার নিকট হইতে এক শত টাকা ধার লইয়াছি I have borrowed one hundred rupees from him (lit. from near him).

ii. Sometimes the ablative is used in an instrumental sense with the verb হওন; as

তোমা হইতে যে এত হইবে ইহা কে জানিত Who would have thought that this would be done by you?

This is like such English expressions as 'one would not expect such treatment *from* you.'

iii. The colloquial termination থেকে is used with inanimate objects; as

আমি বাগান থেকে আসিয়াছি I have come from the garden.

কলিকাতা থেকে কাশী পর্য্যন্ত From Calcutta to Benares.

iv. The terminations of the locative এ, এতে, তে, and য় (see pp. 16, 18) are used to indicate the source whence anything is produced, or the material of which it is made. Native grammarians regard this as an ablative, though it may equally well be looked on as a locative; as

এ ক্ষেত্রে শস্য জন্মে In or from this field corn is produced.

খনিতে ধাতু পাওয়া যায় In or from the mine metal is found or obtained.

মৃত্তিকায় পুত্তলিকা হয় The doll is made of clay.

§ 21. THE GENITIVE (সম্বন্ধ).

This case is used in two ways; first, as a possessive indicating possession or relation; secondly, as the form adapted for affixing postpositions.

i. As a possessive it is used in the same way as in other languages, but it should be borne in mind that the genitive precedes the noun which governs it; as

রামের পুস্তক Rām's book.

তাঁহার পিতার ঘর His father's house.

Owing to the paucity of adjectives denoting the material of which a thing is made in the colloquial language, the genitive is used where in English an adjective would be employed; as

কাষ্ঠের রথ A wooden car (lit. a car of wood).

লৌহের দণ্ড An iron rod (lit. a rod of iron).

সোণার চুড়ী A golden bracelet (lit. a bracelet of gold).

ii. With postpositions, as mentioned at p. 64, the genitive precedes; as

তোমার প্রতি Towards you.

ঘরের উপর Upon the house.

ইহার ভিতর মানুষ থাকে Some one is inside this (place).

But with ভিন্ন, ছাড়া, বই, and similar words, the nominative is used; as

ধার্ম্মিক ভিন্ন অন্যে সুখী হইতে পারে না None but the religious man can be happy.

সে ছাড়া আর কেহ আমাকে সাহায্য করিতে পারে না No one but he can help me.

iii. To express necessity, duty, obligation, the verb is put in the infinitive followed by হওন, and requires either the genitive or dative of the person affected; as

তাহাকে ফৌজদারী আদালতে হাজির হইতে হইয়াছিল He had to be present at the Criminal Court.

তোমার সেখানে যাইতে হয় You ought to go there.

আমি বাবুর মহিনা খাই সুতরাং তাঁহার কায আমাকে করিতে হয় I take (lit. I eat) the Bābu's wages, consequently I must do his work.

তিনি আমার বন্ধু আমাকে তাহার রক্ষা করিতে হবে He is my friend, I am bound to protect him.

সে আমার গলায় পড়িছে কাযে কাযে আমার তাহার হয়ে বলিতে হল He fell on my neck, therefore I was obliged to speak in his behalf.

In this construction the genitive and dative may almost be used indifferently; if there is any distinction between them it is that the dative is used when necessity or compulsion is implied, the genitive when duty or moral obligation is involved. The dative, in other words, means 'must,' and the genitive means 'ought.' The distinction, however, seems to be rather theoretical than practical, and does not appear to be always strictly observed.

iv. The infinitive with আছে, as mentioned at p. 55, implies

the power to do, or the option of doing, and takes either the genitive or dative, as in the instance given at the page quoted above.

v. With the negative verb নাই the construction with the genitive implies prohibition from custom or religion; as

ত্রয়োদশীর দিন হিন্দু দিগের বেগুন খেতে নাই On the thirteenth day of the month Hindus must not eat brinjals (i.e. they are forbidden by their religion to do so).

vi. Similarly, the verbal noun followed by চাই (see p. 57) takes either the genitive or the dative; as

তোমার or তোমাকে একবার সেখানে যাইতে চাই You ought to go there once.

এ সকল বিষয় তোমার জানা চাই You ought to know all these things.

vii. In respect to vessels, buildings, and receptacles of all sorts there is an important distinction to be observed. In speaking of vessels constructed for, or usually applied to, containing any particular article or material, the name of the article is put in the genitive and precedes that of the vessel; and it matters not whether the vessel be at the time full of that material or empty. In such cases in English we generally use a sort of Tatpurusha compound (see p. 13), as 'a medicine-bottle,' 'a cotton-warehouse;' thus দুধের বাটী 'a milk-can,' তুলার গুদাম 'a cotton-warehouse,' বিচালির নৌকা 'a straw-boat' (i.e. a boat used for carrying straw).

আমি বজরা পেলুম না, কি করি খড়ের নৌকায় এলুম I could not find a passenger-boat, so I was obliged to come in a straw-boat.

আমার মদের বোতলে কি হবে আমি ঔষধের এক টা শিশি চাই What use is a wine-bottle to me, I want a medicine-phial.

If, however, it is meant to imply that the vessel is full, then the noun indicating the vessel is put first, and that indicating the contents last in the nominative. In such constructions a numeral usually precedes; as

এক কলসী ঘী One pot of ghī.

দুই নৌকা চাউল Two boat loads of rice.

If, however, the first noun is repeated, the numeral is omitted; as

কলসী ২ জল তার মাথায় ঢালিলেন তবু তার জ্ঞান হল না। They poured pots and pots of water on his head, but even then he did not recover his senses.

The practice, it will be observed, is precisely the reverse of English. For a vessel intended for a certain purpose we use, in form at least, the nominative, as 'a milk-pot;' while for a vessel full of anything we use the genitive, 'a pot of milk.' So also with areas or measures of space; as

চারি বিঘা জমী Four bighas of land[1].

But when distance is indicated by the time taken in travelling the genitive is used; as

দুই দিনের পথ A two-days' journey.

এক মাসের রাস্তা A month's journey.

viii. Before qualifying adjectives the substantive is put in the genitive; as

কৃষ্ণ সকলের প্রিয় Kṛishṇa is beloved by all.

সে পশুর সমান He is equal to a beast (no better than a beast).

রামের তুল্য পৃথিবীতে আর কেহ নাই There is no one on earth equal to Rāma.

ix. Before the Sanskrit participles ending in তব্য, অনীয়, and য়, signifying 'to be done,' 'that which must be done,' the agent is in the genitive; also before adjectives signifying 'necessary, proper, fit,' and the like; as

এ তোমার কর্ত্তব্য কার্য্য This is your bounden duty.

---

[1] A bigha is the common unit of land measurement. It varies in extent in different districts, but the standard bigha is about one third of an acre.

তিনি দানের যোগ্য পাত্র He is a fit object of charity.

তাহা করা আপনার আবিশ্যক It is necessary for you to do that.

দেব সেবা আপনার করণীয় বটে The worship of the gods must certainly be performed by you (high style).

x. With the numerous Sanskrit past participles so commonly employed in modern Bengali (see p. 44) the agent is put either in the genitive or instrumental; as

এ কাহার কৃত By whom was this done?

রঘুবংশ কালিদাসের or কালিদাস কর্ত্তৃক রচিত The Raghuvanśa (was) composed by Kālidāsa.

In this instance the verb 'to be' is of course understood, but it must be noted that when the verb is expressed the agent must always be in the instrumental; thus it is correct to say

রঘুবংশ কালিদাস কর্ত্তৃক রচিত হইয়াছে,

but incorrect to say

রঘুবংশ কালিদাসের রচিত হইয়াছে.

This peculiar construction arises from the nature of compound verbs, as will be explained in the next paragraph.

xi. The Bengali language being originally a simple rustic speech did not possess primary verbs for expressing the more complicated ideas of civilized life. To meet this want it has had recourse to the practice of making compound verbs by taking a Sanskrit noun and adding to it a simple verb, like কর্ 'to do' and others. The number of such verbs is practically unlimited, as any Sanskrit noun may be so used; and the practice has been extended to modern Bengali nouns also. Now in respect of these verbs there are two methods of construction: (1) When the simple verb is কর্ or a similar active verb the noun with which it is compounded may be regarded as the object of the verb, in which case the person or thing acted upon by the verb is governed by the compounded noun and thus naturally falls into the genitive case; (2) the verb and the noun are regarded as one word, as a simple active verb in fact, and in that case the person acted on is the direct object and is put in the accusative case. Thus if we have to put the following sentence into Bengali we may do it in either of two ways, as shown below:

It is the duty of a king by putting down the wicked, and by protecting the good, to uproot vice and to establish virtue.

(1) রাজার কর্ত্তব্য যে দুষ্টের দমন ও শিষ্টের পালন করিয়া অধর্ম্মের উন্মূলন ও ধর্ম্মের সংস্থাপন করেন.

(2) রাজার কর্ত্তব্য যে দুষ্টকে দমন ও শিষ্টকে পালন করিয়া অধর্ম্মের উন্মূলন ও ধর্ম্মের সংস্থাপন করেন.

In the first of these sentences দমন and পালন are regarded as accusative cases governed by the verb করিয়া; thus দুষ্টের and শিষ্টের naturally become genitives governed by them again. But in the last sentence দমন করেন is regarded as one verb, as a consequence of which the object দুষ্টকে is put in the accusative. It is in fact merely a question of the amount of connexion that is felt to exist between the verb and the noun with which it is compounded. If this connexion is so close that the two words are regarded as forming only one verb, then the object must of course go into the accusative, whereas if the two words are regarded as separate, the noun governed by the verb, then equally of course the preceding noun is governed by the other and falls into the genitive[1].

But the case is different when the verb হওন is employed, as then the genitive alone can be used, হওন being a neuter verb and

[1] The two constructions can hardly be elucidated by English owing to the want of inflexional terminations, but if we use an inflexional language like Latin, they are easily distinguished; thus (1) Regis officium est ut improborum suppressionem et bonorum protectionem faciendo injustitiam tollat et justitiam sustineat. (2) Regis officium est ut improbos supprimendo et bonos protegendo etc. The Latin may not be very classical, but the contrast of the two constructions comes out very clearly.

as such being incapable of governing an object in the accusative case; thus

তাহার আগমন হইয়াছে He has arrived (lit. of him the coming has taken place).

আজি আমার বেড়ান হইল না To-day I have not been for a walk (lit. to-day of me the walking has not been).

§ 22. THE LOCATIVE (অধিকরণ).

The principal use of this case is to indicate the place or condition in which a person or thing is; as

(*a*) of place:

তিনি গৃহে আছেন He is in the house.

সে বাড়ীতে কত জন ধরিতে পারে How many men can go into (be contained in) that house?

তাহার মনে বড় ক্লেশ হইয়াছে He has had great trouble in his mind.

(*b*) of condition:

বৃষ্টির অভাবে কৃষকের কার্য্যে ব্যাঘাত হইয়াছে Owing to the absence of rain the business of cultivation is impeded (lit. *in* the business of the cultivator there is impediment).

ওই সৌদাগর এখন সুখে আছে That merchant is now well off (lit. *in* prosperity is).

i. The locative is used in cases where in English the dative or accusative would be used, i.e. 'in' is used for 'on' or 'into' or 'to'; as

তুমি কালিকাতায় কবে যাইবে When will you go *to* (lit. *in*) Calcutta?

রাজা সিংহাসনে উঠিলেন The king ascended the throne (lit. mounted *in*).

বৈষ্ণবী পুষ্পোদ্যানে প্রবেশ করিল The Boishṇabī entered into the garden.

আমাকে কিছু দিলে জলে পড়িবে না If you give me something, it will not be lost (lit. will not fall in the water).

ii. It is also used to indicate the time when anything happened; as

এ মাসের দশম দিবসে এক সভা হইবেক On the tenth of this month there will be a meeting.

এমন সময়ে হলধর উপস্থিত হইয়া বলিল At that time Haldhar presented himself, and said ....

iii. Adverbs of motion and place and the like are used in the locative; as

ধীরে২ চল Move slowly!

নিকটে আইস Come near!

দূরে থাক Stand off! (remain at a distance!)

iv. Verbs implying stopping, sticking, touching, affecting take the locative; as

নৌকা চড়ায় লাগিল The boat stuck on a shoal.

এ কথা তাহার মনে লাগিয়াছিল This saying stuck in his mind.

Such words are commonly used to describe attacks of sickness; the part affected being put in the locative and the person affected in the genitive; as

তাহার মাতায় বড় লাগিয়াছে It (the disease) has attacked him badly in the head.

সে আপন পায় আপনি কুড়ালি মারিয়াছে He himself has struck the axe on his own foot. (This is a proverbial saying, meaning 'he has brought his misfortunes on himself.')

But when no part of the body is named the person affected is in the dative; as

তাহাকে বড় লাগিয়াছে It has attacked him badly.

v. Fitness, skill, appropriateness, and necessity take the locative of the art or business concerned; as

তিনি লেখাতে বড় নিপুণ He is very skilful in writing.

তাহাতে আমার আবশ্যক কি What need have I of that?

সে অনেক বিশয়ে উপযুক্ত He is fit, or qualified, for several things.

আপনি বড় কার্য্যে দক্ষ Your honour is very expert in business.

§ 23. GENERAL RULES.

Under this head are grouped together a number of rules which cannot appropriately be placed under any of the cases, because in some instances one case is used, in others another. Some of these rules, too, refer more to the use of the verb than the noun.

i. As a general rule postpositions require the genitive, but certain ideas may be expressed either by a genitive with a postposition or by some other case without a postposition; as

মাটীতে রাখ (coll.) or
মাটীর উপর রাখ } Put (it) on the ground.

আমার এক খান ঘুড়ি তোমাদের ছাতে or ছাতের উপর পড়িয়াছে My kite has fallen on your roof (lit. of me one piece kite etc.).

Thus, union or disunion may be expressed either by the genitive followed by সহিত, সঙ্গে, or some postposition of similar meaning, or by putting both the objects united in the locative; as

আমার সহিত উহার মিল ছিল or
আমাতে উহাতে মিল ছিল } Between me and him there was friendship.

If the nouns are in the plural, then the genitive with মধ্যে is used; as

আমাদের ও উহাদের মধ্যে এখন বিরোধ যাইতেছে Between us and them at present a quarrel is going on.

When the absence of any difference is implied then the locative is used; as

হরিতে ও হরতে কিছু ভেদ নাই There is no difference between Hari and Hara.

When comparison is made between two persons or objects, the first object is in the nominative or whatever other case may be required by the construction of the sentence, and the second is in the genitive followed by সঙ্গে or simply in the genitive followed by the word denoting comparison or equality; thus

অন্য কবি কালিদাসের সঙ্গে তুল্য হইতে পারে না No other poet can be equal to, or compared with, Kālidās; or

অন্য কবি কালিদাসের তুল্য হইতে পারে না.

But when such equality is denied, both nouns are put in the locative; as

ইহাতে উহাতে সমান নাই Between this one and that one there is no resemblance, or equality. (Vulgo এতে ওতে সমান নয়.)

So also with exchange the locative is used, though colloquially also the genitive with the postposition; as

তোমার ঘড়িতে আমার ঘড়িতে বদল কর or

তোমার ঘড়ি আমার ঘড়ির সঙ্গে বদল কর Exchange your watch for mine.

ii. Some illustrations of the use of the verbal nouns were given at p. 51, par. xvi. The following further rules should be noted:

The verbal noun in আ or ওয়া is used to all intents and purposes as a substantive, to imply the act of doing or being, followed by the verbs হওন, আছি, or থাকন; as

আসা যাওয়া না থাকিলে প্রণয় থাকে না Without intercourse there can be no friendship (lit. coming and going not having been, friendship does not remain).

তোমার এমন কথাটা বলা উচিত হয় নাই It is not proper for you to say such a thing (lit. of you such a word the speaking proper is not).

সে খানে যেই যাওয়া সেই আসা, থাকা হইবে না You must go there and come away at once, you will not stop (lit. there what is going, that is coming, stopping there will not be).

তোমার লেখা দেখিতে চাই I wish to see your writing.

It is used also in the genitive and locative; as

তাহার যাওয়ার কথা শুনিয়া দুঃখিত হইয়াছি On hearing of his going I was sorry.

সে খানে যাওয়াতে কোন দোষ নাই There is no harm in going there.

আমার এই কথা বলাতে তিনি রাগিয়া উঠিলেন On my saying that word he rose up in wrath.

The use of the verbal noun in ন or ণ is so rare that it is not necessary to give any examples. That of ইবা is similar to আ or ওয়া.

iii. Nouns in apposition are of course put in the same case, as গঙ্গা নদী 'the river Ganges,' আম্র ফল 'a mango fruit;' but when two or three nouns in apposition are put in the genitive or any other case, the case termination is added only to the last of them; as

গঙ্গা নদীর তীরে On the banks of the Ganges.

দায়ভাগলেখক জীমূতবাহনের ব্যবস্থা সকারণ The decisions of Jīmūtavāhana the author of the Dāyabhāga are important.

ভারতচন্দ্র রায় গুণাকরে অনেক গুণ ছিল In Bhāratchandra Rāy (surnamed) the Mine of Virtues there was much merit.

These are in the high literary style, but the rule applies also to the ordinary colloquial style; as

ডাক্টর বাবুকে ডাক Call the Doctor Bābu.

কারিকর মোহনের ঠাকুরবাড়ী ভাল Mohan the architect's temple is good.

ছুতোর মিস্তরী কালার কায মন্দ নহে Kālā carpenter's work is not bad.

iv. It has already been stated on p. 25 that the adjective is invariable, and does not change for gender, number, or case. Theoretically, however, the adjective in this, as in most languages, does agree with its substantive, and in consequence when a Sanskrit adjective is used, some writers make it change according to the gender of the substantive. This refinement may as a general rule be neglected by the student, but as he will sometimes find Sanskrit feminines used, the following brief note may be useful:

Sanskrit adjectives ending in ইন্ make the masculine in ঈ and the feminine in ইনী; thus জ্ঞানী পুরুষ 'a learned man,' জ্ঞানিনী স্ত্রী 'a learned woman.'

Adjectives ending in বৎ and মৎ make the masculine in বান and মান and the feminine in বতী and মতী respectively; as রূপবান মনুষ্য 'a beautiful man,' রূপবতী স্ত্রী 'a beautiful woman;' শ্রীমান রাজা 'a fortunate king,' শ্রীমতী রাণী 'a fortunate queen.'

শ্রীমতী is commonly used as a title by ladies of rank, and even as a mere prefix to names of females of all kinds. It corresponds almost to the English 'Mrs.' In legal documents this title will often be found written শ্রীমত্যা, which is really the Sanskrit genitive. This custom arises from the habit, common in former times, of signing one's name to a document in the Sanskrit genitive. The whole signature was, in fact, a Sanskrit sentence beginning with the words পত্রম্ ইদম্ 'this (is the) writing' of so-and-so. Thus also দেবী, the title of Brahman ladies, and দাসী, that of ladies of other castes, are often written দেব্যা and দাস্যা respectively.

v. When two or more nouns are connected together by a conjunctive conjunction, such as 'and,' 'also,' the verb is put in the plural; as

রাম, শ্যাম ও কৃষ্ণ বারাণসী গমন করিয়াছেন Rām, Shyām, and Kṛishṇa have gone to Benares.

But if connected by a disjunctive, as 'or,' 'either,' the verb is in the singular; as

রাম কিম্বা শ্যাম যিনি আসিবে তাহাকে লইয়া আসিবে Rām or Shyām, whichever of them comes, bring with you.

আমি বা আমার ছেলেই যেই যাবে I or my boy will go.

Colloquially, it is more usual in this case to repeat the verb; as

টাকাই থাকুক বা ধান থাকুক নিয়ে আসিবে Be it money or be it rice, bring it.

vi. When a verb is governed by several nouns, each of which, though plural in meaning, is singular in form, the verb is in the singular; as

আলু পাটোল বেগুন বাঙ্গালায় জন্মে Potatoes, cucumbers, and brinjals grow in Bengal.

But if the nouns are followed by a numeral or a plural pronoun, the verb is in the plural; as

ব্রাহ্মণ ক্ষত্রী বৈগু এ তিনি পৈতা ধরেন Brahmans, Kshattris, and Boidyas, these three wear the sacred thread.

ইংরাজী বাঙ্গালী কাবুলী আরবী ইহারা সকলেই কলিকত্তায় বাস করেন English, Bengalis, Kabulis, Arabs, all these live in Calcutta.

vii. Adjectives, when used as substantives, are regularly declined; as

জ্ঞানির সংসর্গে থাকিও Remain in the society of the wise.

মাতালকে শ্রদ্ধা হয় A drunken man tells the truth (lit. to the drunken belief there is).

But when a pronoun is used adjectivally it cannot be declined unless the particle টি or টা is added; as এটা, genitive এটার; কোনটি, accusative কোনটিকে, etc.

§ 24. STRUCTURE OF SENTENCES (পদবিন্যাস).

The order in which words are arranged in a sentence is a matter of much importance, as in this respect the Bengali language differs very widely from English. The two leading rules are: (1) the finite verb is put at the end of a sentence, and (2) every governed word precedes the word which governs it. Owing to the operation of these two rules it frequently happens that the order of words in a Bengali sentence is precisely the reverse of English.

i. The order of words in a simple sentence is: subject—object—verb. In English it is: subject—verb—object; as

রাম শ্যামকে ধরিলেন Rām seized Shyām.

But where a particular word is emphatic, it is put last; as

আগে আমাকে তিনি মারিলেন পরে আমি তাহাকে মারিলাম

First *he* beat me, afterwards I beat him.

Here the speaker wishes to draw attention to the fact that he committed the assault under provocation, because the other man beat him first. The emphasis is therefore on তিনি, and it is therefore put after আমাকে.

তিনি শিখান আমাকে, আমি শিখাই তাঁহাকে He teaches *me*, and I teach *him*.

Here the emphasis is on the persons taught, they are therefore put last.

আগে বলিলেন তিনি, পরে বলিলাম আমি First *he* spoke, then I spoke.

Here attention is drawn to the order in which the persons spoke, the two nominatives which carry the emphasis are put at the end of the respective clauses.

In sentences intended to be satirical, jocose, or angry, the verb is often put first; as চল্‌লেন্ শর্ম্মা 'the great Paudit is going off (in a rage)!' করে বস্‌লেন এক কীর্ত্তি 'he has done a glorious thing indeed!' said satirically when a man is very proud of having done something which was not successful after all (lit. having done one glory he sat).

ii. When an active verb has two objects, one of which is in the accusative and the other in the dative, the dative is put first and the accusative, without termination, next (see § 18, par. iii); as

আমি তাহাকে কিছু বলিতে চাই I wish to say something to him. See also the examples in the above-quoted section.

iii. A qualifying adjective precedes the substantive which it qualifies, but a descriptive adjective is put last; as বুদ্ধিমান ব্যক্তি 'a wise person,' but এই ব্যক্তি বুদ্ধিমান 'this person (is) wise.' In the latter sentence a verb is understood, but rarely expressed. When it is expressed it is put last; as

বুদ্ধিমান লোকের নিকট চাকর থাকিলে সেও বুদ্ধিমান হয় From being the servant of clever people, he also is (has become) clever.

উমেশ অতি শিষ্ট হয়েন Umesh is very polite.

Colloquially, however, the omission of the verb is more usual; as তুই বড় দুষ্ট 'you are very wicked,' সে নির্লজ্জ 'he (is) shameless.' When the verb understood is আছি the adjective may either precede or follow, but the construction with the adjective preceding is more literary than colloquial; as

রাজা দশরথের চারি পুত্র ছিলেন, তন্মধ্যে জ্যেষ্ঠ রাম, মধ্যম ভরত, তৃতীয় লক্ষ্মণ, কনিষ্ঠ শত্রুঘ্ন King Daśaratha had four sons, of these the eldest was Rāma, the next Bharata, the third Lakshmaṇa, the youngest Śatrughna.

Here it would be equally correct to say রাম জ্যেষ্ঠ etc.

iv. The governed word precedes the word which governs it; thus, not only does the genitive precede the governing word (§ 21, par. i), but the object of an active verb precedes the verb, an adverb of time or place precedes the verb and takes the first place in the sentence or clause, except when it governs a noun, in which case the noun goes first. The result of these rules is, that a Bengali sentence has often to be read into English backwards. Instances of the genitive preceding have been given above, and will be found frequently throughout this work. The following are instances of the location of the adverb:

কালক্রমে বানুও পণ্ডিত হইবেন In time even Bānu will become a learned man. (Bānu is a rustic lout.)

এই গ্রামের প্রান্তভাগে এক মন্দির ছিল, তাহাতে এক যোগী তপস্যা করিতেন, এক্ষণে সে মন্দির নষ্ট ও সে যোগী অদৃষ্ট হইয়াছেন *On the outskirts* of this village there was a temple, *there* a Jogi used to perform penance, *now* that temple is destroyed and the Jogi has disappeared.

The words in italics are adverbs, and take the first place in their respective clauses, except the first, which is preceded by the word 'village,' which it qualifies.

The two following passages, in high literary style, will illustrate the arrangement of words in a sentence, with reference to all the foregoing rules. It will be observed that they are composed almost entirely of Sanskrit words, with only just so much Bengali as is necessary to bind them together. Nine-tenths of these grand words would be utterly unintelligible to the masses:

কনিষ্ঠ যুবারাজ আপন বৃদ্ধ পিতাকে অত্যন্ত অপমানপূর্ব্বক দৃঢ় নিগাড় বদ্ধ ও মহা ঘোর কারাগারে রুদ্ধ করিয়া বলে রাজ্যাধিকার ও সিংহাসনারোহন করিয়াছেন।

Literally:

The youngest prince (his) own old father excessive disgrace-preceded strong fetters-in bound, and very dreadful prison-in confined having-made, force-by kingdom-power and throne-ascending made.

In ordinary English this would run thus:

The youngest prince having bound his aged father in fetters in a most disgraceful manner (or, with every mark of disgrace), confined him in a dreadful prison, and by force took possession of the kingdom, and ascended the throne.

এক দিবস তাঁহারা দুই বন্ধুতে ভ্রমণার্থ নির্গমন কালীন অনতিদূরস্থ এক কাত্যায়নীর মন্দিরে শ্রবণমনোহর বীণাশব্দ শ্রবণ

করিয়া কৌতুকাবিষ্ট চিত্তে সত্বরে তথায় উপস্থিত হইয়া দেখিলেন এক পরম সুন্দরী কন্যা বীণানুগত স্তুতিগর্ভ গীত দ্বারা ভগবতী কাত্যায়নীর আরাধনা করিতেছেন।

One day they two friends for the sake of walking going-forth time not-very-far-standing one Kātyāyanī-of temple-in hearing-pleasant flute-sound hearing having made, curiosity-possessed mind-with there quickly present having been, saw a very beautiful maiden flute-accompanied praise-containing song-by goddess Kātyāyanī-of worship is making.

Or in ordinary English:

One day the two friends when they went out for a walk heard the sweet sounds of a flute from a temple of Kātyāyanī close by. Urged by curiosity they quickly went there, and saw a very beautiful maiden worshipping the goddess Kātyāyanī with a song of praise to the accompaniment of a flute.

Many examples of this kind of long involved sentence will be found in the extracts from official papers contained in this work. The best modern writers, however, now avoid these cumbrous constructions, and write in short sentences.

v. The relative and correlative pronouns and adverbs correspond to one another in the first and second clauses of a sentence. Where the first clause opens with any of the relatives whose type is য (see pp. 35, 59), the second clause must open with the corresponding relative whose type is স or ত. Thus to যিনি answers তিনি, to যে answers সে, and so on; as

যিনি জীবন দিয়াছেন তিনি আহার দিবেন He who has given life, (He) will give food.

যে ব্যক্তি এমত কর্ম্ম করিয়াছে সে ব্যক্তি সব করিতে পারে The man who has done that, (that man) can do everything.

যাহা মন্দ তাহা হেয় Whatsoever is bad, (that) is contemptible.

যখন তুমি যাইবে তখন আমিও যাইব Whenever you go, (then) I also will go.

তুমি যেখানে থাকো সেখানে মনুষ্য থাকিতে পারে না Where you dwell, there no man can dwell.

বৈকুণ্ঠ যেমন জগদীশ তেমন নয় Such as Boikuṇṭh is, such is not Jagadish (i. e. Jagadish is not equal to Boikuṇṭh).

Although, however, the pronoun in the second clause must be the correlative of that in the first clause, it is not necessary that it should be in the same case; it must, of course, take the case required by the construction of the clause. It is, at the same time, thought more elegant, if not more correct, so to word the sentence that the correlative shall be in the same case as the relative; thus it is not incorrect to say,

যে ব্যক্তি আসিবে তাহাকে আমি দান দিব Whoever shall come, to him I will give gifts;

but it would be more elegant to say,

যে ব্যক্তি আসিবে সে দান পাইবে Whoever shall come, he shall get gifts,

because in both clauses the pronoun is in the nominative.

Occasionally, for the sake of emphasis or impressiveness, the correlative sentence is placed first; as

তিনিই যথার্থ পণ্ডিত যিনি বিদ্বান ও ধার্ম্মিক He is a true Pandit, who is wise and virtuous.

Sometimes the relative is omitted, and sometimes the correlative, but the former is rare, and chiefly in poetry; as

সকল প্রাণিকে দেখে আপনার মত।
সেই সে পণ্ডিত হয় শাস্ত্রের সম্মত॥

(He who) regards all living things as equal to himself,
He is that sage approved by the Shastras.

তুমি যাহা খাইতে চাও দিব Whatever you wish to eat, (that) I will give.

যাহা বল কিন্তু আমার মনে সন্দেহ জন্মিয়াছে Whatever you say, still doubt has arisen in my mind.

In the first instance the relative is omitted *metri gratiâ*. It should be যে সকল etc.; in the two last the correlative is omitted—তাহা দিব etc. and তাহা হইলেও.

The relative যে is sometimes colloquially inserted in hasty or half-interjectional sentences; thus, to the question 'where is Rām?' the answer might be, সে যে বাড়ী গিয়াছে 'why, he has gone home.' I can only translate যে by 'why,' uttered in a tone of surprise. It is, in fact, almost untranslateable, though the construction is extremely common.

vi. It may be useful here to give a list of certain words which, by the usage of the language, correspond to each other, so that when one is used in the first clause of a sentence the other must be used in the last.

যদি if,	requires	তবে then.	
যদ্যপি যদিও যদিস্যাৎ	although,	,,	তথাপি তত্রাপি তথাচ	yet, still, nevertheless.
বরং বরঞ্চ	rather,	,,	তথাপি না তত্রাপি না তবু না	yet not (than).
হয় either,	,,	নয় or.	
নয় neither,	,,	নয় nor.	
না neither,	,,	না nor.	
অপেক্ষা চেয়ে	than,	,,	বরং বরঞ্চ	rather.

Some of these words are used in such a way that it is difficult to find exact English equivalents for them. বরং, for instance means 'good,' and বরঞ্চ is the same word with the Sanskrit চ 'and' added to it (বরংচ). হয় is the verb 'is,' and নয় the negative of the same; thus

যদি তুমি যাও তবে আমি যাই If you go, then I go.

যদ্যপি তুমি আমার মন্দ করিয়াছ তথাপি আমি তোমার মন্দ করিব না Although you have done ill by me, I will do no ill by you.

বরং প্রাণ হারাইব তবু মান হারাইব না I will rather lose my life than my honour (lit. better *or* rather I will lose my life, then I will not lose my honour).

বরং শূন্য গোয়ালি ভাল তবু দুষ্ট গরু ভাল নয় Better is an empty cowshed than a vicious cow. (Proverb; lit. rather an empty cowshed good, then a vicious cow is not good.)

হয় যাও নয় থাক Either go, or stay (lit. (if) it is, go; (if) it is not, stay).

নয় ভাল নয় মন্দ Neither good, nor bad (lit. it is not good, it is not bad).

সে না হিন্দু না মুসলমান He is neither Hindu nor Musulman.

উহা অপেক্ষা বরং ইহা ভাল This is better than that (lit. than that rather this is good).

মন্দ পুত্র হওয়ার চেয়ে বরং পুত্র না হওয়া ভাল It is better to have no son at all than a bad son (lit. than the being of a bad son, rather a son not being is good).

It will be seen from the above instances that the negative is often used in the sense of 'or.' Thus, to express the idea 'are you going or shall you stay here?' they would say, 'do you go? no? do you stay?' This construction is colloquially very common.

vii. When a long string of nouns is used to govern one verb, or to form one sentence, the conjunctive conjunction should, strictly speaking, be inserted after each one of them, but in modern usage this has been felt to be cumbrous, and it is now more common to insert the conjunction only between the two last, or even to omit it altogether; as

যুধিষ্ঠির ও ভীম ও অর্জুন ও নকুল ও সহদেব এই পাঁচ ভাই পঞ্চ পাণ্ডব or

যুধিষ্ঠির, ভীম অর্জুন নকুল ও সহদেব etc. Yudhishṭhira, Bhima,

Arjuna, Nakula, and Sahadeva, these five brothers are the five Pāṇḍavas.

viii. When two or more nouns in the genitive case are joined by a conjunction, the termination may optionally be added to both, or only to the last; as

শাক্ত ও বৈষ্ণবের মধ্যে দ্বেষ আছে or
শাক্তের ও বৈষ্ণবের etc. Between Śāktas and Vaishṇavas there is enmity.

But when both nouns are in the accusative, it is more common to add the termination only to the last; as

মহেশ কিম্বা ভুবনকে এখানে পাঠাইয়া দিও Send Mahesh or Bhuban here.

When the conjunction is ও, the termination may be added to both nouns. The same rule applies to adjectives when declined as substantives (see § 23, par. vi); as

জ্ঞানি গুণি ও মানিকে আদর কর Reverence the wise, the virtuous, and the venerable.

Though less usual, it would not be incorrect to say জ্ঞানিকে etc. This rule does not apply to pronouns, which must always have the case terminations; as

তোমাকে ও তাঁহাকে যাইতে হইবে You and he must go.

To say তোমা ও তাঁহাকে would be incorrect.

ix. Interrogation is colloquially indicated merely by the tone of the voice, as in other languages. In writing, also, the English sign of interrogation is now frequently used; thus তুমি যাবে? 'will you go?'

But, for the sake of greater clearness, কি is often introduced, either before or after the verb; thus তুমি কি যাবে or তুমি যাবে কি. Or the verb is put first; as যাবে তুমি or যাবে কি তুমি.

When the fact is already known and the question is put merely to compel a confession, or to clench an argument, না or না কি is used; as

তুমি না সেখানে গিয়াছিলে Did not you go there?

রাজা নাকি গুলি খাইয়া মরিয়াছে Was not the Rājā killed by a bullet? (lit. did not the Rājā having eaten a bullet die?)

x. In conversation, and occasionally also in writing, the substantive verbs আছে and হওন in the present tense are omitted, being understood. This is peculiarly the case in short sentences, where the meaning is perfectly clear without them; as

তোমার নাম কি What (is) your name?

তিনি উত্তম লোক He (is) a very good man.

So also, but less frequently, with the imperfect ছিলাম, and the preterite of হওন; as

যখন পলাশির যুদ্ধ হয় তখন আমি কাশীতে omitting ছিলাম When the battle of Plassy took place, I (was) at Benares.

তিনি গত omitting হইয়াছে He (is) gone.

আমার এখন বড় সুখ omitting হইয়াছে I am now very happy.

It is difficult to lay down exact rules for the omission or insertion of the substantive verb. It is so much a matter of habit and custom that no native grammarian seems to have considered it worth analysing. It is necessary to realise the difference in meaning of the two verbs. Those who know Sanskrit will readily understand it by bearing in mind that আছে is the Sanskrit অস্, while হওন is Sanskrit ভূ; for others, the matter may be made clear by observing that there are in many Aryan languages two verbs meaning 'to be,' one of which is a mere copula or linking-word used to connect other words in a sentence where no special stress is laid on the idea of being, while the other is used when the idea of being is an important element in the sentence[1]. The former is often

---

[1] The best example of this distinction in modern languages is the use of *ser* (esse) and *estar* (stare) in Spanish.

omitted, its existence being so readily understood. Thus, where an adverb is used emphatically in a sentence, it draws the attention to itself, and the verb is taken for granted, as আমি এখন ব্যস্ত 'I am *now* busy;' but if the adverb is omitted, the verb is inserted, as আমি ব্যস্ত আছি 'I am busy.' So also when speaking familiarly, or when addressing an inferior, brevity or a tone of command is expressed by omitting the verb; as তুই কি 'who (are) you?' The latter is more generally inserted, though when the adjective is used descriptively, as explained in par. iii above, it is omitted. Thus it is inserted in

কই তিনি দুঃখিত হন নই Where is he not grieved? i.e. of course he is grieved.

কোথায় তিনি দুঃখিত হবেন Where will he be grieved? i.e. of course he will be pleased.

But it is omitted in

যে সকল লোক শীতে কাতর তাহাদিগের কাপড় দেওয়া উচিত To those who are suffering from cold, it is proper to give clothes.

তিনি অতি বুদ্ধিমান ব্যক্তি He is a very clever person.

CHAPTER VII.

SPECIMENS OF BENGALI LITERATURE.

I.

Short Sentences.

যে সর্বাবস্থায় সন্তুষ্ট সেই সুখী।

কুসংসর্গে থাকা অপেক্ষা একাকী থাকা ভাল।

স্বর্ণের পরীক্ষা অগ্নীতে বন্ধুর পরীক্ষা বিপদে।

মূর্খের অন্তঃকরণ মুখে জ্ঞানির মুখ অন্তরে।

যে কখনো দুঃখে পড়ে নাই সে সুখের স্বাদ পায় নাই।

দুঃখ যে সহিতে পারে না সে অত্যন্ত দুঃখী।

ভাবিয়া করিও যেন করিয়া ভাবিও না।

যার জন্যে করিবে চুরি সেও বলিবে চোর।

পাপ করিলে ভুগ্‌তে হয়।

তোমার মতন উপযুক্ত লোক কজন পাওয়া যায়।

গতিক বড় ভাল নয় বোধ হয় সর্বনাশ হইবে।

পরিশ্রম করিলে রত্ন মিলিবে।

তুমি কি মনে করেছ সংসারে থেকে ধর্ম্ম কর্ম্ম করিবে।

মূর্খের অনেক দোষ তাই বলি ভাল করিয়া লেখা পড়া শিখ।

ডুব দিয়া জল খেলে কারও সাধ্য নাই যে ধরে।

কায করিতে গেলে মন চাই নহিলে কি কাজ ভাল হয়।

টাকা পাইলে খরচ করিতে ইচ্ছা হয়।

মরিতে হবে বলিলে লোকে কি কখনো হিংসা করে।

দুষ্ট লোককে সকলেই ঘৃণা করে।

১০ মানুষ হলেই লোকে সুখ্যাতি করে॥

II.

Short Sentences.

আশাকে সংযমন করা সুখী হইবার প্রধান উপায়।

বিজ্ঞ লোক অন্যের দোষ দৃষ্টে আপন দোষ সংশোধন করেন।

অন্যের দোষ দেখিবার সময় আমাদের চক্ষুঃ সতেজ কিন্তু আপন দোষ দেখিবার সময় অন্ধ।

সুবাক্যে পর আত্মীয় হয় দুর্বাক্যে আত্মীয় পর হয়।

5 সম্পদে স্বার্থসাধন নিমিত্ত অনেকে বন্ধু হয় কিন্তু বিপদে কেহ থাকে না।

পণ্ডিত লোক ধার্ম্মিকের প্রশংসা করেন অবশিষ্ট লোক ধনির ও পরাক্রান্তের প্রশংসা করেন।

অপরিমিত ব্যয়ী আপন উত্তরাধিকারিকে ফাকি দেয় কৃপন আপনাকে বঞ্চিত করে।

সজ্জনের হৃদয় নবনী হইতেও কোমল কেমনা নবনী আপনি উত্তাপ না পাইলে দ্রব হয় না সজ্জনের মন অন্যের তাপ দেখিয়া দ্রব হয়।

পণ্ডিতের শস্ত্র শাস্ত্র, মূর্খের শস্ত্র অস্ত্র।

10 যে কর্ম্ম একবার করিলে আর ফিরিবে না তাহা বিলক্ষণ বিবেচনা পূর্ব্বক করিও।

সাহসে কোন কার্য্যে প্রবৃত্ত হওয়া উচিত নহে।

উদ্যোগী পুরুষ প্রায়ই লক্ষ্মীবন্ত হইয়া থাকে।

মনুষ্যের অহঙ্কার তুল্য শত্রু নাই।

পবিত্র মানবদেহে কেন পাপের সঞ্চার হইবে।

স্বভাবজ বনজাত শাক দ্বারা ও উদর পরিপূর্ণ করা যাইতে পারে।

উন্নত হইতে ইচ্ছা করিলে অগ্রে নম্র হইতে হয়।

পরদুঃখে যে হৃদয় কাতর নহে সে মনুষ্য পদ বাচ্য নহে।

ধার্ম্মিক হইলে লোকে শ্রদ্ধা করিয়া থাকে।

আশ্চর্য্য এই যে লোকে ধনক্ষয়ে দাসকে ক্রয় করে তথাপি মিষ্ট বাক্যে স্বাধীনকে কিনিয়া রাখে না।

জীব সৃষ্টি করিবার পূর্ব্বে জগদীশ্বর আহার প্রস্তুত করিয়া রাখেন ॥

III.

Dialogue between Two Countrymen.

(ভেরি বাদ্য শুনিয়া)

১ম চাষা। মামা গো ওডা ভোঁ ভোঁ কল্লে আর কি বলে গো মামা।

২য় চাষা। তুই অ্যাও জানিস্ নি ওড়া তুরি না তুরি কি বলে যে আর যো লোকটা বেজ্‌য়ে বেজ্‌য়ে বেড়াচ্চে ওর নাম আজ হুড।

১ম চাষা। কি এক খামা বলয়ে যে।

২য় চাষা। রোস সেমুজে দেখি। বোজ্‌লাম রে বোজ্‌লাম সবনাশ কল্লে গালাম আর কি। আজার বেটা আম চন্দের এক খামা নোতুন পুয়ে করবে তাই মোদের জেনয়ে দিচ্চে তা

ঋদি আজ একবার আজার বেটা পুন্নে করে তবেই তো মোরা ত্যালাম মোদের ছু লায় পা দেওয়া হোলো ছু আয়গায় থাজনা দে কোন স্মুন্দী ফসল কত্তি পারে রে।

(ভট্টাচার্য্য মহাশয়কে দেখিয়া)

১ম চাষা। ভটচন্ধি মুশাই পরনাম গো। এ লোকটি ঝা বল্যে মোদের সেম্‌জে ত্যান তো॥

From রাম বনবাস a drama, by Manamohana Basu.

IV.

The Villager in Trouble about his Land.

সাধুচরণের বাড়ী

লাঙ্গল লইয়া রাইচরণের প্রবেশ॥

রাই। (লাঙ্গল রাখিয়া) আমিন সুমুন্দি ত্যান বাগ। যে রোক করে মোর দিকে আস্‌ছিলো। বাবা রে! মুই বলি মোরে বুঝি খালে। সোঁপালতলার ৫ কুড়ো ভুঁই যদি নীলি ত্যাল তবে মাগ্‌ ছেলেরে খাওয়াব কি। কাঁদাকাটি করে ত্যাকুবো যদি না ছাড়ে মোরা কাজেই ত্যাশ ছাড়ে যাব।

ক্ষেত্রমণির প্রবেশ

দাদা বাড়ী এয়েছে?

ক্ষেত্র। বাবা বাবুদের বাড়ী গিয়েছে আলেন আর দেরি নেই কাকীমারে ডাক্‌তি যাবা না? তুমি বক্‌চো কি?

রাই। বক্‌চি মোর মাতা। একটু জল আন্‌দিনি খাই তেষ্টায় যে ছাতি ফেটে ত্যাল। সুমুন্দিরি ক্যাত বল্লাম তা কিছুটি শোন্‌লে না।

সাধুচরণের প্রবেশ এবং ক্ষেত্রমণির প্রস্থান।

সাধু। রাইচরণ তুই এত সকালে বাড়ী এলি?

রাই। দাদা আমিন শালা সোঁপালতলার জমিতি দাগ মেরেচে খাব কি বচ্ছেরে যাবে কেমন করে। আহা জমি তো না জান সোনার চাঁপা। এক কোন্ কেটে মহাজন কাৎ কত্তাম। খাব কি ছেলে পিলে খাবে কি। এতডা পরিবার না খাতি পেয়ে মারা যাবে ও মা! রাত পোয়ালি যে দু কাটা চালির খরচ, না খাতি পেয়ে মর্‌বো আরে পোড়া কপাল, আরে পোড়া কপাল!

সাধু। জল খা, জল খা, ভয় কি, জীব দিয়েচে যে আহার দিবে সে॥

From নীল দর্পণ a play, by Dinabandhu Mitra. Act i. sc. 2.

V.

A Rich Man's Country House.

কুন্দ, নগেন্দ্রদত্তের সঙ্গে গোবিন্দপুরে আসিল। কুন্দ, নগেন্দ্রের বাড়ী দেখিয়া অবাক্ হইল।

এত বড় বাড়ী সে কখন দেখে নাই। তাহার বাহিরে তিন মহল, ভিতরে তিন মহল। এক একটি মহল এক একটি বৃহৎ পুরী। প্রথমে, যে সদর মহল, তাহাতে এক লোহার ফটক দিয়া প্রবেশ করিতে হয়, তাহার চতুষ্পার্শ্বে বিচিত্র উচ্চ লোহার রেইল। ফটক দিয়া তৃণশূন্য প্রশস্ত, রক্তবর্ণ সুনির্ম্মিত পথে যাইতে হয়। পথের দুই পার্শ্বে, গোগণের মনোরঞ্জন, কোমল নবতৃণবিশিষ্ট দুই খণ্ড ভূমি। তাহাতে মধ্যে মধ্যে মণ্ডলাকারে রোপিত, সকুসুম, পুষ্পবৃক্ষ সকল বিচিত্র পুষ্পপল্লবে শোভা

পাইতেছে । সম্মুখে বড় উচ্চ দেড়তালা বৈঠকখানা । অতি প্রশস্ত সোপানারোহণ করিয়া তাহাতে উঠিতে হয় । তাহার বারেণ্ডায়, বড় বড় মোটা ফ্লুটেড্ থাম; হর্ম্ম্যতল মর্ম্মরপ্রস্তরাবৃত । আলিশার উপরে, মধ্যস্থলে এক মৃণ্ময় বিশাল সিংহ জটা লম্বিত করিয়া, লোল জিহ্বা বাহির করিয়াছে । এইটি নগেন্দ্রের বৈঠকখানা । তৃণপুষ্পময় ভূমিখণ্ডদ্বয়ের দুই পার্শ্বে, অর্থাৎ বামে ও দক্ষিণে দুই সারি একতালা কোঠা । এক সারিতে দপ্তরখানা ও কাছারি । আর এক সারিতে তোষাখানা এবং ভৃত্যবর্গের বাসস্থান । ফটকের দুই পার্শ্বে দ্বাররক্ষকদিগের থাকিবার ঘর । এই প্রথম মহলের নাম "কাছারি বাড়ী" । উহার পার্শ্বে "পূজার বাড়ী" । পূজার বাড়ীতে রীতিমত বড় পূজার দালান; আর তিন পার্শ্বে প্রথমত দোতালা চক বা চত্বর । মধ্যে বড় উঠান । এ মহলে কেহ বাস করে না । দুর্গোৎসবের সময়ে বড় ধুমধাম হয়, কিন্তু এখন উঠানে টালির পাশ দিয়া ঘাস গজাইতেছে । দালান, দরদালান, পায়রায় পূরিয়া পড়িয়াছে, কুঠারি সকল আসবাবে ভরা,—চাবি বন্ধ । তাহার পাশে ঠাকুরবাড়ী । সেখানে বিচিত্র দেবমন্দির, সুন্দর প্রস্তরবিশিষ্ট "নাট-মন্দির," তিন পাশে দেবতাদিগের পাকশালা, পূজারিদিগের থাকিবার ঘর এবং অতিথিশালা । এই তিন মহল সদর । এই তিন মহলের পশ্চাতে তিনমহল অন্দর । কাছারি বাড়ীর পশ্চাতে যে অন্দর মহল, তাহা নগেন্দ্রের নিজ ব্যবহার্য্য । তন্মধ্যে কেবল তিনি, তাঁহার ভার্য্যা ও তাঁহাদের নিজ পরিচর্য্যায় নিযুক্ত দাসীরা থাকিত । এবং তাঁহাদের নিজ ব্যবহার্য্য দ্রব্য সামগ্রী থাকিত । এই মহল নূতন, নগেন্দ্রের নিজের প্রস্তুত; এবং তাহার নির্ম্মাণ অতি পরিপাটি । তাহার পাশে পূজার

বাড়ীর পশ্চাতে সাবেক অন্দর। তাহা পুরাতন, কুনির্ম্মিত; ঘর সকল অনুচ্চ, ক্ষুদ্র এবং অপরিষ্কৃত। এই পুরী বহুসংখ্যক আত্মীয় কুটুম্বকন্যা, মাসী, মাসীত ভগিনী, পিসী, পিসীত ভগিনী, বিধবা মাসী, সধবা ভাগিনেয়ী, পিসীত ভাইয়ের স্ত্রী, মাসীত ভাইয়ের মেয়ে, ইত্যাদি নানাবিধ কুটুম্বিনীতে কাকসমাকুল বটবৃক্ষের ন্যায়, রাত্রি দিবা কল কল করিত। এবং অনুক্ষণ নানাপ্রকার চীৎকার, হাস্য পরিহাস, কলহ, কুতর্ক, গল্প, পরনিন্দা, বালকের হুড়াহুড়ি, বালিকার রোদন, “জল আন” “কাপড় দে” “ভাত রাঁধলে না” “ছেলে খায় নাই” “দুধ কই” ইত্যাদি শব্দে সংক্ষুব্ধ সাগরবৎ শব্দিত হইত। তাহার পাশে ঠাকুর বাড়ীর পশ্চাতে, রন্ধনশালা। সেখানে আরো জাঁক। কোথাও কোন পাচিকা ভাতের হাঁড়িতে জ্বাল দিয়া পা গোট করিয়া, প্রতিবাসিনীর সঙ্গে তাঁহার ছেলের বিবাহের ঘটার গল্প করিতেছেন। কোন পাচিকা বা কাঁচা কাঠে ফুঁ দিতে দিতে ধুঁয়ায় বিগলিতলোচনা হইয়া, বাড়ীর গোমস্তার নিন্দা করিতেছেন, এবং সে যে টাকা চুরি করিবার মানসেই ভিজা কাঠ কাটাইয়াছে, তদ্বিষয়ে বহুবিধ প্রমাণ প্রয়োগ করিতেছেন। কোন সুন্দরী তপ্ত তৈলে মাছ দিয়া চক্ষু মুদিয়া, দশনাবলী বিকট করিয়া, মুখভঙ্গি করিয়া আছেন, কেন না তপ্ত তৈল ছিটকাইয়া তাঁহার গায়ে লাগিয়াছে; কেহ বা স্নানকালে বহু-তৈলাক্ত, অসংযমিত কেশরাশি, চূড়ার আকারে সীমন্তদেশে বাঁধিয়া তালে কাটি দিতেছেন।।

From বিষবৃক্ষ or ‘The Poison Tree,’ by Bankim Chandra Chatterjea. Chap. vii.

VI.

Letter of a Deserted Wife.

শোকের প্রথম বেগ সম্বরণ হইলে, কমলমণি পত্র খুলিয়া পড়িলেন। পত্রখানির শিরোনামায় তাঁহারই নাম। পত্র এইরূপ;—

"যে দিন স্বামীর মুখে শুনিলাম যে আমাতে আর তাঁর কিছুমাত্র সুখ নাই, তিনি কুন্দনন্দিনীর জন্য উন্মাদগ্রস্ত হইবেন, অথবা প্রাণত্যাগ করিবেন, সেই দিনেই মনে মনে সঙ্কল্প করিলাম, যদি কুন্দনন্দিনীকে আবার কখন পাই, তবে তাহার হাতে স্বামীকে সমর্পণ করিয়া তাঁহাকে সুখী করিব। কুন্দনন্দিনীকে স্বামী দান করিয়া আপনি গৃহত্যাগ করিয়া যাইব; কেন না, আমার স্বামী কুন্দনন্দিনীর হইলেন, ইহা চক্ষে দেখিতে পারিব না। এখন কুন্দনন্দিনীকে পুনর্ব্বার পাইয়া তাহাকে স্বামী দান করিলাম। আপনিও গৃহত্যাগ করিয়া চলিলাম।

"কালি বিবাহ হইবার পরেই আমি রাত্রে গৃহত্যাগ করিয়া যাইতাম। কিন্তু স্বামীর যে সুখের কামনায় আপনার প্রাণ আপনি বধ করিলাম, সে সুখ দুই একদিন চক্ষে দেখিয়া যাইবার সাধ ছিল। আর তোমাকে আর একবার দেখিয়া যাইব সাধ ছিল। তোমাকে আসিতে লিখিয়াছিলাম—তুমি অবশ্য আসিবে, জানিতাম। এখন উভয় সাধ পরিপূর্ণ হইয়াছে। আমার যিনি প্রাণাধিক, তিনি সুখী হইয়াছেন ইহা দেখিয়াছি। তোমার নিকট বিদায় লইয়াছি। আমি এখন চলিলাম।

"তুমি যখন এই পত্র পাইবে, তখন আমি অনেক দূর যাইব। তোমাকে যে বলিয়া আসিলাম না, তাহার কারণ এই

যে, তা হইলে তুমি আসিতে দিতে না। এখন তোমাদের কাছে আমার এই ভিক্ষা যে, তোমরা আমার সন্ধান করিও না।

"তোমার কাছে জন্মের মত বিদায় হইলাম, আশীর্ব্বাদ করি, তোমার স্বামী পুত্র দীর্ঘজীবী হউক। তুমি চিরসুখী হও। আরও আশীর্ব্বাদ করি যে, যে দিন তুমি স্বামীর প্রেমে বঞ্চিত হইবে, সেই দিন যেন তোমার আয়ুঃশেষ হয়। আমায় এ আশীর্ব্বাদ কেহ করে নাই॥"

Ibid. Chap. xxviii.

VII.

An Unscrupulous Attorney.

বাবুরাম বাবুর টাকাতে অতিশয় মায়া—বড় হাত ভারি—বাক্স থেকে টাকা বাহির করিতে হইলে বিষম দায় হয়। মহাজনদিগের সহিত কচ্‌কচি ঝক্‌ঝকি করিতেছেন, ইতিমধ্যে প্রেমনারায়ণ মজুমদার আসিয়া উপস্থিত হইলেন এবং কলিকাতার সকল সমাচার কাণে২ বলিলেন। বাবুরাম বাবু শুনিয়া স্তব্ধ হইয়া থাকিলেন—বোধ হইল যেন বজ্র ভাঙ্গিয়া তাঁহার মাথায় পড়িল। ক্ষণেক কাল পরে সুস্থির হইয়া ভাবিয়া মোকাজান মিয়াকে ডাকাইলেন। মোকাজান আদালতের কর্ম্মে বড় পটু। অনেক জমিদার নীলকর প্রভৃতি সর্ব্বদা তাহার সহিত পরামর্শ করিত। জাল করিতে—সাক্ষী সাজাইয়া দিতে—দারোগা ও আমলাদিগকে বশ করিতে—গাঁতের মাল লইয়া হজম করিতে—দাঙ্গা হাঙ্গামের জোটপাট ও হয়কে নয় করিতে নয়কে হয় করিতে তাহার তুল্য আর এক জন পাওয়া ভার। তাহাকে আদর করিয়া সকলে ঠকচাচা বলিয়া ডাকিত, তিনিও

তাহাতে গলিয়া যাইতেন এবং মনে করিতেন আমার শুভক্ষণে জন্ম হইয়াছে—রমজান ইদ সোবেরাত আমার করা সার্থক—বোধ হয় পিরের কাছে কসে ফয়তা দিলে আমার কুদ্‌রৎ আরও বাড়িয়া উটিবে । এই ভাবিয়া একটা বদনা লইয়া উজু করিতে ছিলেন, বাঞ্ছারাম বাবুর ডাকাডাকি হাঁকাহাঁকিতে তাড়াতাড়ি করিয়া আসিয়া নির্জ্জনে সকল সংবাদ শুনিলেন । কিছুকাল ভাবিয়া বলিলেন—ডর কি বাবু? এমন কত শত মকদ্দমা মুঁই উড়াইয়া দিয়েছি—এবা কোন্ ছার? মোর কাছে পাকা২ লোক আছে—তেনাদের সাথে করে লিয়ে যাব—তেনাদের জবানবন্দিতে মকদ্দমা জিত্‌ব—কিছু ডর কর না—কেল্ খুব ফজরে এসবো, এজ্ চল্লাম ॥

From আলালের ঘরের দুলাল or 'The Spoilt Child of the House of Alāl,' by Tekchand Thākur (Piāri Chand Mitra). Chap. v.

VIII.

The Rake's Progress.

মতিলাল ক্রমে২ মেরোয়া হইয়া উঠিল, এমনি ধূর্ত্ত হইল যে পিতার চক্ষে ধুলা দিয়া নানা অভদ্র ও অসৎ কর্ম্ম করিতে লাগিল । সর্বদাই সঙ্গিদিগের সহিত বলাবলি করিত বুড়া বেটা একবার চোক বুজলেই মনের সাদে বাবুয়ানা করি । মতিলাল বাপ মার নিকট হইতে টাকা চাহিলেই টাকা দিতে হইত—বিলম্ব হইলেই তাহাদিগকে বলে বসিত—আমি গলায় দড়ি দিব অথবা বিষ খাইয়া মরিব । বাপ মা ভয় পাইয়া মনে করিতেন কপালে যাহা আছে তাই হবে এখন ছেলেটি প্রাণে বাঁচিয়া থাকিলে আমরা বাঁচি—ও আমাদিগের শিব রাত্রির

শলিতা—বেঁচে থাকুক, তবু এক গণ্ডুষ জল পাব। মতিলাল ধুমধামে সর্ব্বদাই ব্যস্ত—বাটীতে তিলার্দ্ধ থাকে না। কখন বনভোজনে মত্ত—কখন যাত্রার দলে আকড়া দিতে আসক্ত—কখন পাঁচালির দল করিতেছে—কখন সকের দলের কবিওয়ালাদিগের সঙ্গে দেওরা২ করিয়া চেঁচাইতেছে—কখন বারওয়ারি পূজার জন্য দৌড়াদৌড়ি করিতেছে—কখন খেম্টার নাচ দেখিতে বসিয়া গিয়াছে—কখন অনর্থক মারপিট, দাঙ্গা হাঙ্গামে উন্মত্ত আছে। নিকটে সিদ্ধি, চরস, গাঁজা, গুলি, মদ অনবরত চলিয়াছে—গুডুক্ পালাই২ ডাক ছাড়িতেছে। বাবুরা সকলেই সর্ব্বদা ফিট্ফাট্—মাথায় ঝাঁকড়া চুল—দাঁতে মিসি—সিপাই পেড়ে ঢাকাই ধুতি পরা—বুটোদার এক্লাই ও গাজের মেরজাই গায়—মাথায় জরির তাজ—হাতে আতরে ভুরভুরে রেসমের হাতরুমাল ও এক২ ছড়ি—পায়ে রুপার বগ্লসওয়ালা ইংরাজি জুতা। ভাত খাইবার অবকাশ নাই কিন্তু খাস্তার কচুরি, খাসা গোল্লা, বরফি, নিখুতি, মনোহরা ও গোলাবি খিলি সঙ্গে২ চলিয়াছে॥

Ibid. Chap. ix.

IX.

A Sylvan Scene.

লক্ষ্মণ কহিলেন আর্য্য! এ দিকে দণ্ডকারণ্যভূভাগ অবলোকন করুন। এই স্থানে দুর্দ্ধর্ষ কবন্ধ রাক্ষসের বাস ছিল। এই এ দিকে পম্পা সরোবর। রাম পম্পা শব্দ শ্রবণে সীতাকে সম্বোধন করিয়া কহিলেন, প্রিয়ে পম্পা পরম রমণীয় সরোবর। আমি তোমার অন্বেষণ করিতে২ পম্পাতীরে উপস্থিত হইলাম। দেখিলাম প্রফুল্ল কমল সকল মন্দ মারুত ভরে ঈষৎ আন্দোলিত

হইয়া সরোবরের অনির্ব্বচনীয় শোভা সম্পাদন করিতেছে। উহাদের সৌরভে চতুর্দ্দিক আমোদিত হইতেছে। মধুকরেরা মধুপানে মত্ত হইয়া গুন গুন স্বরে গান করিয়া উড়িয়া বেড়াইতেছে হংস সারস প্রভৃতি বহুবিধ বারিবিহঙ্গগণ মনের আনন্দে নির্ম্মল সলিলে কেলি করিতেছে॥

From সীতার বনবাস by Pandit Ishwara Chandra Vidyāsāgara.
Chap. i. p. 19.

X.

Sītā's Lament.

এই বলিতে২ জানকীর কণ্ঠরোধ হইয়া গেল। তিনি কিয়ৎ ক্ষণ বাক্য নিঃসরণ করিতে পারিলেন না; অনন্তর দীর্ঘ নিশ্বাস পরিত্যাগ পূর্ব্বক কহিলেন। লক্ষ্মণ, আমি জন্মান্তরে কত মহাপাতক করিয়াছিলাম বলিতে পারি না নতুবা বিধাতা আমার কপালে এত দুঃখভোগ লিখিবেন কেন? বিধাতারই বা অপরাধ কি সকলে আপন২ কর্ম্মের ফল ভোগ করে আমি জন্মান্তরে যেমন কর্ম্ম করিয়াছিলাম এ জন্মে সেইরূপ ফল ভোগ করিতেছি। বোধ করি পূর্ব্ব জন্মে কোনও পতিপ্রাণা কামিনীকে পতিবিয়োজিতা করিয়া ছিলাম সেই মহাপাপেই আজ আমার এই দুরবস্থা ঘটিল নতুবা আর্য্যপুত্রের হৃদয় স্নেহ দয়া ও মমতায় পরিপূর্ণ। আমিও যে একান্ত পতিপ্রাণা ও শুদ্ধচারিণী তাহাও তিনি বিলক্ষণ জানেন। তথাপি যে এমন সময়ে আমায় পরিত্যাগ করিলেন সে কেবল আমার পূর্ব্বজন্মার্জ্জিত কর্ম্মের ফল ভোগ॥

Ibid., p. 55.

XI.

A Charge of Theft laid at a Police Station.

জেলা হরিপুর থানা নবথালি

বাদী . . . রাম কৃষ্ণ দাস
আসামী . . . কৃষ্ণ দাস
সাং তাঁতীবন্দর } মোকদ্দমা. দঃ বিঃ ৩৮০

১৯ নং জানুয়ারি
১৮৯১ সাল }

আমি শ্রী রাম কৃষ্ণ দাস বৈরাগী পেঃ ৺ কৃষ্ণ চৈতন্য দাস বৈরাগী ষ্টেশনে উপস্থিতে এজাহার করিতেছি যে গত বুধবারের দিন রাত্রি আমার বাটীতে একটা অতিথি যাইয়া রাত্রিতে থাকিতে চাহায় আমি তাহাকে খাওয়াইয়া আপন গায়ের পুরাতন ১ খানা লুইয়ের কাপড় তাহাকে গায় দিতে দিয়া দক্ষিণ দ্বারী খোলা ঘরের মধ্যে আমি ও সে শুইয়া ঘুমাইয়া গিযাছিলাম; রাত্রি দুই দণ্ড থাকিতে উঠিয়া দেখিলাম যে আমার নিকট শুইয়া থাকা অতিথিটি নাই, খালি বিছানা পড়িয়া আছে এবং আমার একটা পিতলের কমণ্ডলু তথায় ছিল, তাহা নাই, তখন চারি দিক তল্লাস করিয়া না পাইয়া, তল্লাসে গিয়াছিলাম, দুই দিন পরে বাড়ি আসিয়া মহল্লার সমির সেখ চৌকীদারকে বলিয়া এতক তল্লাস করিতেছিলাম, পাই নাই; তাহার নাম তখন কৃষ্ণ দাস ও বাড়ি প্রথম বনগ্রাম পরে তাঁতীবন্দর বলিয়াছিল; সে আর কোন দিন আমার বাড়ী যায় নাই সেও বৈরাগী বলিয়া পবিচয় দিয়াছিল, তাহার সঙ্গে একটা আঁচলা

ও একটা হুঁকা এবং একখানা কাশ্মীরী ছিল, আমার ঐ লুইয়ের দাম এক্ষণে ১, একটাকা হইবে; ছেঁড়ে নাই, ২ স্থানে ইন্দুরে কাটার সেলাই করা ও আড়ে দুই মুড়া কান্ ফিতা দিয়া মুখে সেলাই আছে। ও কমণ্ডলু আন্দাজ /১ এক সের ঘি /১। সওয়া সের আছে, তাহার মূল্য ।৹ আনা হইবে। আমার এজাহার এই, আমি লেখা পড়া জানি; নিজের নাম লিখিতে পারি, তদন্তের প্রার্থনা রাখি ইতি।

বাদীকে এই এজাহার পাঠ করিয়া শুনাইলে ঠিক থাকা কহিল ইতি॥

XII.

A Charge of Theft laid at a Police Station.

জেলা হরিপুর থানা করিমাবাদ

বাদী রাম নারায়ণ ঘোষ	সাং চালুতে তলা	মোঃ দঃ ৩৭৯|৪১১
আসামী কাকি সেখ	„ তোলাইপুর	ধারা

৫ নং জানুয়ারি
১৮-৯১ সাল

আমি শ্রী রাম নারায়ণ ঘোষ বয়স ২৪|২৫ বৎসর, পিতা রামেশ্বর ঘোষ সাং চালুতে তলা ১২ নং বীট্; ১২ নং বুধুই সেখ চৌকীদার সহ আপনার নিকট জমসেরপুর গ্রামে রাত্রি ১০ টার সময়, রাইটার কনষ্টেবলের পত্র দাখিল করিয়া এই এজাহার করিতেছি যে আমার একটি ছিটের কোট ... দা

পিরান্ আজ্ ৬ দিন হইল আমার পূর্ব্ব দ্বারী আল্‌গা ঘরে রাখিয়াছিলাম গত পরশু তারিখে আমার খুড়া গোপীনাথ ঘোষ গোয়াড়ি যাওয়াতে, তিনি লইয়া গিয়াছেন, মনে করিয়াছিলাম; কল্য রাত্রিতে আমার ঐ খুড়া বাড়ী আসায় তাঁহাকে জিজ্ঞাসা করায় তিনি লইয়া যান নাই বলেন, তখন ঐ পিরান ও কোট ঐ তারিখের মধ্যে কোন দিন চুরি হওয়া জানিয়া বুধুই চৌকী-দারকে কহিয়া তল্লাস করিতেছিলাম; আজ্ প্রাতে মটর গাছ কিনিতে তোলাইপুর যাই, তথায় পরাণ বিশ্বাসের বাড়ির কাছে বসিয়াছিলাম। সেই সময় ঐ তোলাইপুর সাকিনের কাকি সেখ আমার চুরি যাওয়া কোট্‌টি গায় দিয়া আসিতে থাকায় আমার চুরি যাওয়া কোট্ চিনিয়া ধরি; কাকি সেখ কহে ঐ কোট্ তাহার ছোট ভাই গায় দিতে দিয়াছে, এই কোট্ কাহার তাহা জানে না। আমড়ে গ্রামের পুলিন ও বিপিন ঘোষের নিকট রাখিয়া টেঁপিদহ গ্রামের চৌকীদারকে ডাকিতে যাই তথায় আমড়ে গ্রামের বুধুই সেখ চৌকীদারকে ও টেঁপিদহ গ্রামের চিনি সেখ চৌকীদারকে পাইয়া ডাকিয়া আনি এবং কাকি সেখকে, মোকদ্দমা করিব না, দে ভাই আমার সাদা পিরানটি; তাহাতে ঐ কাকি সেখ চাল্‌তেতলার কড়ঙ্গ সাহা, তোলাই পুরের মছুর মণ্ডল, এবাদ সেখ, ফকীর মাল্‌তে, হাজি মাল্‌তে প্রভৃতির সাক্ষাতে ঐ সাদা পিরানটি ঘর হইতে বাহির করিয়া দেয় তাহাতে ঐ কাকি সেখ, আমার নিম্নের তালিকার লিখিত ৸৹ ৬ মূল্যের কোট্ পিরান চুরি করা জানিয়া চৌকীদার সহ ষ্টেশনে র‍্যাঃ কঃ কে সংবাদ দিয়া তাঁহার পত্র লইয়া আপনার নিকট আসিয়া এই এজাহার করিলাম। প্রতিবাদীর উপর দাবী ও দণ্ডের প্রার্থনা করি; ঐ কোট মজলিসপুরের ব্রজেন্দ্র

নাথ চৌধুরী দিয়াছিল ও পিরানটি নাটনার কলিমদ্দিসেখ সেলাই করিয়া দিয়াছিল, ঐ মাল যে আমার তাহা ব্রজেন্দ্র চৌধুরী কলিমদ্দি খলিফা, কুঞ্জ দাস ও রাম গোপাল চৌধুরী চিনিবেক ॥

XIII.

A Charge of Burglary laid at a Police Station.

জেলা হরিপুর থানা আলমপুর

বাদী . . . রাম চন্দ্র সীংহ   সাং লতিভোজা

আসামী . . . অজ্ঞাত

দঃ বিঃ ৪৫৭ ধারা, সিঁদ চুরি

৯ নং মার্চ
১৮৯১ সাল

আমার নাম রাম চন্দ্র সীংহ পেঃ সেবক সীংহ পূর্ব্ববাস কলিকাতা, ভবানীপুর হাং বাস লতিভোজা মহল্লার চৌকীদার ভরুস সেখ সহ পঞ্চাইতের এতেলা দাখিল করিয়া এজাহার করিতেছি যে গত রাত্রিতে আমার উত্তর দ্বারী ঘরের মধ্যে আপন পরিবার সহ শুইয়াছিলাম, রাত্রি ১ টার সময় ঘরের মাচার উপর হইতে চোর বাক্স নীচে নামান শব্দ শুনিয়া আমার পরিবারের ঘুম ভাঙ্গিয়া আমাকে জাগাইলে, ঘর তখন অন্ধকার ছিল,—১ টি লোক সিঁদ দিয়া বাহির হইয়া যায় ঐ লোকটিকে চিনিতে পারি নাই, বাহিরে আর কেহ ছিল কিনা বলিতে পারি না; আলো জ্বালিয়া দেখি আর একটি বাক্স

ঐ মাচায় ছিল, ঐ বাক্‌সের তালা খোলা, মধ্যস্থিত কাঁসার পানের বাটায় থাকা ও কাঁসার গেলাসে থাকা নগদ টাকা পয়সা সিকি দুয়ানি, ১০, টাকার হিসাবে ২ কেতা নোট, মাল আদি নিম্নের মাল চোরে চুরি করিয়া লইয়া গিয়াছে; লতি-ভোজার প্রহ্লাদ বিশ্বাসের সহিত আমার মনান্তর আছে, তাহার যোগাযোগে চুরি হইয়াছে। সোণার চিক আদি রূপার মল তাবিজ আদি চোরে নামান বাক্‌সে থাকায় লইতে পারে নাই। রত্রিতে চৌকীদার পাহারা দিয়া গেলে এই ঘটনা হইয়াছে, আমার এজাহার এই লেখা পড়া জানি না, এজাহার পাঠ করাইয়া শুনাইলে কহিল ঠিক লেখা আছে॥

XIV.

Petition of a Village Watchman.

মহামহিম জেলা হরিপুরের শ্রীল শ্রীযুক্ত মাজিষ্টার সাহেব
বাহাদুর প্রবল প্রতাপেষু

দরখাস্ত শ্রী হিরুলাল ঘোষ বরখাস্ত চৌকিদার সাং গোবিন্দ পুর অধিনের নিবেদন এই যে আমি ইতি পূর্ব্বে চৌকিদারি কার্য্যে নিযুক্ত থাকিয়া বিশেষ সুখ্যাতির সহিত কার্য্য করিয়া আসিতেছিলাম। আমার অটল ঘোষ নামক একটী সহোদর ভ্রাতা আছে; দৈবাধীন সে এক জন দুষ্ট লোকের পরামর্শে মিলিয়া অদ্য প্রায় ৭ সাত বৎসর হইল একটী চুরি মোকদ্দ-মায় আশামী হইয়া ২ দুই বৎসর কয়েদ সাজা পায় তাহার পর এ পর্য্যন্ত সে আর কোন রূপ দুষ্কর্ম্মের কার্য্য করে নাই

ও তাহার সেই স্বভাব সংশোধন হইয়া গিয়াছে আমি বুঝিতে পারিতেছি। প্রায় ৪|৫ মাস অতীত হইল পূর্ব্বস্থিত শ্রীযুক্ত ডিঃ মুঃ সাহেব বাহাদুর এক সময়ে মোরখালী থানায় ইনস্পেকশন করিতে আসিয়া আমি উক্ত কয়েদ খালাশী অটল ঘোষের সহোদর ভ্রাতা জানিতে পারিয়া আমাকে চৌকিদারী কার্য্যে নিযুক্ত রাখা ভাল নহে বিবেচনা করিয়া মোরখালী থানায় শ্রীযুক্ত সব ইঃ বাবুকে আমাকে বরখাস্ত করার প্রার্থনার রিপোর্ট দিতে আদেশ করেন মোরখালীর পূর্ব্বস্থিত সব ইঃ বাবু লাল বিহারী রায় অধিনের বিরুদ্ধে বিপোর্ট করায় চৌকিদারী সেরেস্তার ভার প্রাপ্ত ডেপুটী মাজিঃ রায় বাহাদুর আমাকে চৌকিদারী কার্য্য হইতে ডিসমিস্ করিয়াছেন। হুজুর আমি গরিব লোক চাকরিটী ছিল বলিয়া কোন রূপ প্রকারে দিন গুজরান করিয়া আসিতেছিলাম, হটাৎ চাকরিটী যাওয়ায় আমার বড় কষ্টে দিন গুজরান করিতে হইতেছে। এক্ষণে অন্য উপায় না দেখিয়া আমার উক্ত ভ্রাতার চরিত্র সংশোধন হওয়ার স্বত্বে ও অদ্য হইতে আমি পৃথক হইয়া অন্য বাড়িতে বাস করিতেছি ও ঐ চাকরি পাইবার প্রার্থনায় প্রায় ১ মাস গত হইল মোরখালীর বর্ত্তমান সব ইঃ বাবুর নিকট এক দরখাস্ত করিয়াছি এ পর্য্যন্ত তাহার কোন হুকুম না পাওয়ায় হুজুরে অত্র দরখাস্ত দ্বারায় প্রার্থনা দয়া করিয়া গরিবকে চৌকিদারী দিয়া প্রতিপালন করার পক্ষে বিহিত আদেশ প্রদান আজ্ঞা হয় নিবেদন ইতি সন ১২৯৮ সাল তারিখ ১৬ কার্ত্তিক ॥

XV.

Petition of a Village Watchman.

মহামহিম মহিমাসাগর জেলা হরিপুরের শ্রীল শ্রীযুক্ত
পুলিষ সাহেব বাহাদুর মহিমার্ণবেষু

দরখাস্ত শ্রী বারু শেখ চৌকিদার সাকিন চাপাইগাছী ষ্টেশন মোরখালী জেলা হরিপুর অধিনের কৃতাঞ্জলি পূর্ব্বক নিবেদন এই যে, আমি ছোট বেলা হইতে চৌকিদারী কার্য্য প্রায় ৩০|৩২ বৎসর কাল করিয়া আসিতেছি, প্রথমে এদ্রাক পুরের চৌকিদার ছিলাম পরে বদলী করিয়া চাপাইগাছী গ্রামে দিয়াছিলেন তখন আমার বাটী দয়েরামপুর ছিল, ৩|৪ বৎসর হইল হুজুর হইতে হুকুম প্রকাশ হয় যে, মহল্লায় বাটী না করিলে চৌকিদারী কার্য্য করিতে পারিবেক না, অধিন ঐ হুকুম শিরোধার্য্য করত আমার মহল্লা চাপাইগাছী গ্রামে বসতি বাটী প্রস্তুত করিয়া সপরিবার বস বাস করিয়া সরকারী কার্য্যের আনজাম করিতেছি, ধর্ম্মাবতার ঐ বাটী প্রস্তুত করিতেও আমি কর্জ্জ পত্র করিয়া অনেক ব্যয় করিয়াছি, এবং এত দিবস সরকারী কার্য্য করিয়াছি, কখন কোন অপযশ সরকারে নাই, বরং প্রশংসা আছে। যখন শ্রীযুক্ত বাবু আনন্দ চন্দ্র রায় মোরখালীর ষ্টেশনে সব ইনস্পেকটর তখন সীমলা সাকিমের ঝুড়ান শেখ ও আহ্লাদি পেশাকর দিগের আমার মহল্লার মধ্যে চোর ধরিয়াছি, তাহাদের ২ বৎসর ম্যাদ হয়, এবং ঐ সব ইনস্পেকটর বাবুর আমলে আমার মহল্লার, মেড়েবাদী চলতি চোর ধরি তাহারাও শাস্তি পায়, আর অনেক সময়

আমার ওয়াদার কার্য্যের প্রশংসা পাইয়াছি । বর্ত্তমান সনের শ্রাবণ মাস এই মহল্লার, মুক্ত সুন্দরী দাস্যার ফেলসানি মোকর্দ্দমায় উক্ত বাদিনী আশামীর নিকট টাকা লইয়া মোকর্দ্দমা ছাড়িয়া দিল, ঐ মোকর্দ্দমার সাক্ষি আমি ছিলাম বলিয়া বিনা অপরাধে মহকুমা রামনগরের শ্রীল শ্রীযুক্ত ডেপুটী মাজিষ্ট্রেট বাহাদুর খানাখা আমার উপর রাগান্বিত হইয়া, আমাকে সস্‌পেণ্ড করিয়া রাখিয়াছেন ধর্ম্মাবতার আমি কিদোষে দোষী হইলাম জানিতেও পারিলাম না, আমি এত কাল সবকারী কার্য্য করিয়া বিনা দোষে সসপেণ্ড থাকি বড়ই দুঃখের কথা, তবে আমি গরিব চাকর বলিয়াই এ দুরাবস্থায় পতিত হইয়া রহিয়াছি, আমি যে হুজুরে গিয়া আমার অবস্থা জানাই এমত সঙ্গতি ও নাই, তবে হুজুর এ গরিব চাকরের প্রতি দয়া প্রকাশ করিয়া আমার চাপরাশ দিতে হুকুম হয় কিম্বা আমি কি দোষে দোষী বিচার করিয়া আমার মনের আঁধার ঘুচাইতে আজ্ঞা হয় । উক্ত মোকর্দ্দমার নথী হুজুরে তলব করিলেই সমস্ত বিদিত হইতে পারে ধর্ম্মাবতার কর্ত্তা কৃতাঞ্জলী পূর্ব্বক নিবেদন ইতি সন ১২৯৮|২৬ কার্ত্তিক ॥

XVI.

Petition of Objection in a Revenue Suit.

জেলা হরিপুরের কালেক্টরী আদালত

ছাএল	আপত্তিকারী
শ্রীতারিণী চরণ দাস, অঘোর নাথ দাস,	শ্রীমতি হরি প্রিয়া দেবী অওজে
শ্রীবিনোদ বিহারী দাস ও	শ্রী রামচন্দ্র মুখোপাধ্যায়
শ্রীনাথ দাস	সাং বেলগড়িয়া
সর্ব্ব সাং হরিপুর	

উপরোক্ত আপত্তিকারীর পক্ষে নিম্ন
লিখিত আপত্তি ॥

১। ছাএলগণ ১৯১৬ নং মহাল খরিদ সূত্রে ষোল আনা রকম স্বত্বাংশে ক্ষেমঙ্করী দেব্যার দরুণ মহালে নাম জারি করিবার জন্য যে দরখাস্ত করিয়াছেন তাহাতে তাঁহাদিগের কোন প্রকার নাম জারি করিবার স্বত্বাধিকার নাই।

২। উক্ত ছাএলগণ ও অন্যান্য ব্যক্তি আমার বরাবর উক্ত মহালে পত্তনী জমার খাজানাদি দিয়া দখলীকার আছেন এমতাবস্থায় ছাএলগণ উক্ত মহালে আমার অধীন পত্তনীদার ভিন্ন উক্ত মহালে তাহাদিগের মালিকী কোন স্বত্ব না থাকায় নাম জারী করিবার তাহাদিগের কোন প্রকার অধিকার নাই।

৩। প্রকৃত প্রস্তাবে উক্ত মহালের মূল মালিক ক্ষেমঙ্করী দেব্যা /১২ আনা রকম মালিকী স্বত্ব এবং ৬৭০|৬৭৪|৬৬৫|৬৬৭|

৬৭৭|৭০৬ নম্বর এই সাতটী নম্বর মহালে একত্রে সাধু চরণ সিংহকে ৬২ টাকা পত্তনী জমার বন্দোবস্ত করিয়া উক্ত পত্তনী জমা হইতে তাহার নিজাংশ /১২ গণ্ডা রকমে কালেকটরীর খাজানা উক্ত পত্তনীদারের উপরে বরাত দিয়া তাহাতে স্বত্ববতী ও দখলীকারিণী থাকনাবস্থায় পর লোক গমণ করায় ও তাহার পুত্র সন্তান না থাকায় আমি তাহার এক মাত্র উত্তরাধিকারিণী কন্যা বিধায় আমি উপরোক্ত সমুদয় মহালের পত্তনী জমার উপরোক্ত ছাএল গণের নিকট হইতে খাজানা আদায় পূর্ব্বক স্বত্ববতী ও দখলিকারিণী আছি ছাএলগণ দুরভিসন্ধি মূলে আমার স্বত্বাংশ ধ্বংস করিবার জন্য এই নাম জারি করিবার প্রার্থনা করিয়াছেন প্রকৃত প্রস্তাবে ছাএলগণ পত্তনীদার সাধু চরণ সিংহের বিনামদার মাত্র ॥

XVII.

Statement in a Partition Suit.

জেলা হরিপুরের কালেক্টরী আদালত।

বাদী	প্রতিবাদী
শ্রী রমাকান্ত দাস	শ্রী অম্বিকা কান্ত রায়
সাং জিয়ারথী	সাং জিয়ারথী

১। বাদী যে সম্পত্তী বাঁটোয়ারা জন্য নালিস করিয়াছেন ঐ সম্পত্তি ৫০ বৎসরের অধিক কাল হইতে সকল মালীকগণের অভিপ্রায় ও স্বীকারানুসারে সুবিধা ও অসুবিধা বিবেচনায় জমিবিভাগ ও প্রজাবিলি দ্বারা আপোষে বাঁটোয়ারা হইয়া তদবধি সকল সরিকান নিজ নিজ নির্দ্দিষ্ট অংশে নির্ব্বিরোধে

এ কাল পর্য্যন্ত দখলিকার আছেন। প্রার্থীত বাঁটোয়ারা সম্পত্তিতে মোট ৯ খানি গ্রাম ও জলকর গুজর ঘাট মাথাভাঙ্গা যথাঃ—জিম্মারথী, মেঠপাড়া, কথালীপুর, গোপালপুর, শিরপুর, লক্ষ্মীপুর, পিয়ারপুর, কুস্থারপুর ও য়োড়াগাছা, ইহার মধ্যে কুস্থারপুর ও গোপালপুর প্রভৃতি প্রতিবাদীর ৷৵. অংশ মত ষোল আনা রকমে দখল করিতেছেন এবং মেঠপাড়া, লক্ষ্মীপুর, শিরপুর ও পিয়ারপুর এই চারি গ্রাম ৷৷৵. আনার সরিক দরখাস্তকারীর ষোল আনা রকম উল্লিখিত বিভাগ সূত্রে দখল হইয়া আসিতেছে। ইহাব্যতিত জিম্মারথীতে ভদ্রাসন, ও য়োড়াগাছা গোরাই নদীর তীরস্থ বলিয়া এবং কথালীপুরে হাট থাকা হেতু ও জলকর মাথাভাঙ্গা বিভাগ যোগ্য না থাকা হেতু আমরা সরিকান সকলে আপন আপন অংশমত ঐ তিন গ্রামের জমিও প্রজা ছায় বাঁটোয়ারা সূত্রে পৃথক রূপে ভোগ দখল করিয়া আসিতেছি এক্ষণে একাকী বাদী বাঁটোয়ারা জন্য আইনানুসারে এই নালিস করিতে অধিকারী নহেন॥

XVIII.

Application in a Settlement Case.

মহামহিম

শ্রীযুক্ত হরিপুরের কালেক্টর সাহেব বাহাদুর

বরাবরেষু—

দরখাস্ত শ্রী মহারাজা রাম চন্দ্র দেব বাহাদুর সাঃ

হরিপুর রাজধানী নিবেদন এই যে

১। অত্র কালেক্টরীর তৌজীর ৮৪১ নং চর গোয়ালগ্রাম দরখাস্তকারীর সেবাইতী মালিকী স্বত্ব ভুক্ত মহাল।

২। ১২৭৯ সাল হইতে ১২৮৮ সাল পর্য্যন্ত উক্ত মহাল মিঃ রবার্টস এণ্ড কোম্পানীর সহিত সরাসরি বন্দোবস্ত ছিল ঐ বন্দোবস্ত দরখাস্তকারীর মালিকী স্বত্বাধিকারের অধীন থাকা মহামান্য হাই কোর্ট পর্য্যন্ত আদালত কর্ত্তৃক স্থির হইয়াছে।

৩। উক্ত মহালের গবর্নমেণ্ট রেভিনিউ স্থায়ী বন্দোবস্ত না থাকা বশতঃ সময় সময় সরাসরি বন্দোবস্তের অধীন থাকায় যদি ও উক্ত সাহেবান ১২৭৯ সালে নিলাম খরিদার রূপে বন্দোবস্ত লইয়াছিলেন প্রকৃত পক্ষে উক্ত সাহেবানের বন্দোবস্ত সময়ে দরখাস্তকারীর পক্ষ হইতে গবর্নমেণ্টের দেয় খাজানা উক্ত সাহেবান দরখাস্তকারীর অধীন tenure holder স্বরূপ মারফতদার রূপে সরকারে আদায় করা আদালতের ক্রমান্বয় নিষ্পত্তির দ্বারা গণ্য হইয়াছে॥

XIX.

Petition in a Land Registration Case.

জেলা হরিপুরের কালেক্টরী আদালত

ছায়েল	আপত্তিকারী
শ্রী সোনামনি দাসী	শ্রী হরি মোহন মৈত্র
সাং রামনগর	সাং রামনগর

১১৮ নং সি মহালের নাম জারীর মোকদ্দমা

উক্ত মোকদ্দমার আপত্তিকারী শ্রী হরি মোহন মৈত্রের পক্ষ হইতে আপত্তি করিয়া প্রার্থনা যে নীচের লিখিত হেতুবাদে আপত্তিকারীর নিকট হইতে প্রমাণাদি গ্রহণে দরখাস্তকারীর

প্রার্থনা নামঞ্জুর করিয়া আপত্তিকারীর খরচা দেওয়াইতে আজ্ঞা হয়।

১। ১১৮ নঃ সি মহালে সোনামনি দাসীর কথিত নাবালক পুত্র আশুতোষ দাসের কোন প্রকার নাম জারি কখন না থাকায় এই দীর্ঘ কাল পরে অত্র মহালে তৎস্থলে উক্ত সোনামনি দাসীর নাম জারি হইতে পারে না।

২। উক্ত ১১৮ নং সি মহালে সোনামনি দাসীর বর্ত্তমান পুত্র যোগেন্দ্রনাথ দাস সোল আনা নাম জারি থাকায় ও ছায়েল সোনামনি দাসী তাহাতে সম্মত থাকায় এই নাম জারির প্রার্থনা আদৌ চলিতে পারে না।

৩। আইন ও অবস্থানুসারে সোনামনি দাসী মৃত আশুতোষ দাসের পরিত্যক্ত কোন সম্পত্তিতে স্বত্ববতী দখিলকারিণী কস্মিন কালে হয়েন নাই ও হইতে পারে না। ও তন্মূলে উক্ত মহালে অথবা তাহার কোন অংশে সোনামনি দাসীর কোন প্রকার স্বত্ব দখল না থাকায় তাহার নাম জারির প্রার্থনা আদৌ চলিতে পারে না॥

XX.

A Settlement Proceeding.

রুবকারী বন্দোবস্তী বাবদে আরাজিয়াৎ মওয়া পয়বস্তি চর বাজেআপ্তি বনাম চর দুর্লভপুর লগ্ন মৌজে দুর্লভপুর পরগনে গোয়াস মোতালকে জেলা হরিপুর মহাল খাস সরকার বাহাদুর বিঃ ১৭৯৩ সালের ৮ আইন ও সন ১৮২২ সালের ৭

আইন কর্ত্তৃক শ্রীযুক্ত এফ, টি, প্লাটস্ সাহেব ডেপুটী কালেক্টর জেলা ফরিদপুর মহকুমা ফরিদপুর সন ১৮৬১|২৩ শে এপ্রিল মোং সন ১২৬৮ সাল তাং ১২ বৈশাখ

(১ ধারা এই মহাল বন্দোবস্ত করণে সরকারের কি স্বার্থে কি রূপ অনুমতি হয় তাহার বেওরা)

(১ প্রকরণ মহালের পূর্ব্ব বৃত্তান্ত) এই মহালের পূর্ব্বাবস্থা এই যে, ইত্যগ্রে তরফ বেতাইএর কানুনগো রাম লাল বন্দ্যোপাধ্যায়ের আবেদন পত্রানুযায়ী মৌজে দুর্লভপুরের নীচে খড়িয়া নদী জারি থাকা ও পরে নদীর বেগ পরিবর্ত্তনের দ্বারা পয়বাস্ত হওয়া প্রকাশ হওয়াতে ঐ চর দুর্লভপুরের মকদ্দমা সন ১৮১৯ সালের ২ য় আইনানুসারে শ্রীযুক্ত সাবেক কালেক্টর সাহেবের হুজুরে সরকার বাহাদুর, বাদী লোকনাথ রায়ের প্রতিবাদীত্বে ৪৫ নম্বরে উপস্থিত হইয়া সাহেব মৌছুফের বিচারে সন ১৮৩০ সালের ২৮ শে জানুয়ারী তারিখের ফয়সলার অনুহাত মতে সরকার বাহাদুরের দাবী ডিস্মিস্ হইয়া সন ১৮২৮ সালের ৩ আইনের মর্ম্মানুসারে উক্ত মকদ্দমা সংক্রান্ত সমুদয় কাগজাত চতুর্দ্দশাংশের মহামহিম শ্রীযুক্ত রেবিনিউ কমিসনর সাহেবের হুজুরে প্রেরণ হইলে তথা হইতে রীতিমত খাস কমিসনরি আদালতে সরকার বাহাদুরের তরফ আপীল উপস্থিত হইয়া উক্ত আদালতের হাকিমানের বিচারে প্রসংসিত কালেক্টর সাহেবের ফয়সলা রদ হইয়া আমিনের দ্বারা উক্ত গ্রাম সমুদয়

জরিপ আমলে আসিয়া উক্ত গ্রামের কূইনকূইনি-
য়ালের লিখিত জমি মিলান হইয়া বাকী ২৬৩/৩
বিঘা চর জমির পর সন ১৮৩৩ সালের ২৫
শে জুলাই তারিখে সরকারের আপীল ডিক্রী
হইয়া কর ধার্য্যের অনুমতি হয় ॥

NOTES

TO THE

SPECIMENS OF BENGALI LITERATURE.

I.

THESE are short moral sentences in ordinary language; they present no very great difficulties either of vocabulary or construction.

1. সর্ব্বাবস্থা. This is an example of a compound word such as several Bengali writers are in the habit of creating at pleasure, after the pattern of Sanskrit. It is composed of সর্ব্ব 'all' and অবস্থা 'condition.' In making these compounds the rules of Sandhi (see p. 10) are observed. The student will not find much difficulty in resolving these words into their component parts. A few of the less obvious compounds are given in the glossary.

2. থাকা অপেক্ষা 'than to live,' 'than living.'

7. The strict grammatical construction is in this sentence sacrificed to an epigrammatic neatness of expression. The first ভাব্ means 'consider,' the second 'repent.' যেন 'so that.'

8. বলিবে has here the sense of 'to be called,' 'to be spoken of as,' a sense which this verb not unfrequently bears.

9. ভুগ্তে, colloquial for ভোগিতে, here meaning 'to suffer.' The original meaning of ভোগ্ being 'to feed on,' hence 'to experience;' it is applied both to suffering and enjoyment.

13. করেছ = করিতেছ, থেকে = থাকিয়া.

15. খেলে = খাইলে.

20. মানুষ here in the sense of a brave man—'vir,' not 'homo.'

II.

The sentences in this section are a little more elaborate, and are for the most part in a higher literary style than the preceding. Their structure, however, is simple, and calls for few remarks.

1. আশা here used in the sense of 'expectations.'

2. দৃষ্টে 'by seeing,' for দৃষ্টিতে. আপন used as an adjective, 'their own.'

4. পর, lit. 'other,' here means strangers or even enemies.

10. আর ফিরিবে না 'cannot be altered.'

17. মনুষ্য পদ 'the rank or dignity of manhood;' it means 'he is not worthy to be called a *man* (emphatically).'

III.

This and the following section are written in the ordinary colloquial language of the lower classes, and require a good deal of explanation. They are made to look more difficult than they really are by the author's habit of trying to express the harsh pronunciation of rustics by grotesque combinations of characters.

The subject is taken from the well-known story of Rāma. As he is being proclaimed jubarāj, or heir-apparent, two rustics, hearing the sound of trumpets and proclamations, ask each other what it is all about.

Line 2. মামা গো 'oh! uncle.' কল্লে = করিলে.

4. অ্যাও. This perfectly unpronounceable word is intended to express 'this' (ইহাও) or perhaps 'that' (উহাও); it is not unlike the strange sound a peasant makes in uttering this word. তুরি না ভুরি; তুরি is 'a bugle' and ভুরি is an unmeaning word, such as are often used in describing things vaguely; it is as if he said 'that is a bugle wugle,' i.e. a bugle or something of that kind. কি বলে যে 'what you may call it.'

5. বেজুয়ে = বাজাইয়া 'playing.'

8. রোস = রহিস 'stop.' সেমুজে = সমুঝাইয়া 'having explained.' বোজ্‌লাম = বুঝিলাম 'I understand.'

9. গ্যালাম = গেলাম 'we have gone,' i. e. we are lost, ruined. In order to express the flat sound which এ sometimes has, like the English *a* in *back*, they use long ā with the appended form of য attached to the preceding letter. This curious combination seems in some way to their minds to reproduce the English sound, and they use it accordingly in transliterating English words. আজা and আম are for রাজা and রাম respectively. This omission of the initial consonant is somewhat rare. The author rather overdoes the rudeness of the dialect.

10. কর্‌বে = করিবে 'he will make.' জেনয়ে = জানাইয়া, দিচ্চে = দিতেছে *jānāiyā ditechhe*, 'makes known.'

12. নায় locative case of না for না 'a boat.' হোলো for হইল 'we shall have to place our feet on two boats,' i.e. our position will become very unsafe.

13. সম্বিন্দ for সম্বন্ধী 'a relation,' 'companion,' colloquially 'fellow,' 'chap;' 'a fellow can't raise a crop.' কচ্চি = করিতে.

15. মুশাই a corruption of মহাশয় 'sir.' ঝা = জাহা.

16. ছান = দেন for দেউন. সেমুজে ছান = সমুঝাইয়া দেউন 'please to explain.'

IV.

This is also in rustic speech, but somewhat less extravagant than the preceding.

Line 2. প্রবেশ is the technical word to express the entry of an actor on the scene: 'enter Raicharaṇ carrying a plough.'

3. জ্যান = যেন 'like.'

4. রোক করে 'being angry;' রোক is a corruption of রাগ 'anger.' মুই বলি মোরে বুঝি খালে, this is hardly translateable literally; it means 'I said (to myself) I think he is going to eat me.'

6. ছাহ্‌বো = দেখিব 'let me see,' 'let me try.'

7. ছাশ = দেশ 'country,' here 'my native land,' by which he does not mean the whole of Bengal, but only his own village.

12. মোর মাতা 'my bad luck.' মাতা for মাথা 'forehead;' a man's destiny is supposed to be written on his forehead.

18. বচ্ছরে for বৎসর 'year,' 'in the whole year.' জমি তো না; না here is not negative, but merely emphatic: 'The land, indeed, is like a gold ornament. By cutting off a corner of it I could satisfy the money-lender.'

21. কাটা here means a quantity equal to about two-and-a-half *seers*, or five lbs. 'Every day, as sure as the night passes, two kāṭās or ten pounds of rice are consumed.'

V.

This passage from one of the best works of the leading Bengali novelist Bankim Chandra Chatterjea is in ordinary literary Bengali, with perhaps an extra dash of long Sanskrit words. The style is pure and fluent, and the picture life-like.

Line 4. মহল, lit. 'a dwelling-place,' is used to describe each of the separate wings or buildings composing a large native house. Such a house is a series of courtyards with rooms round them. Each courtyard with the rooms pertaining to it is called a Mahal, and, as the writer well remarks, is like a big town.

8. গোগণের gen. pl. of গো 'a cow.'

9. নবতৃণবিশিষ্ট, one of the long Sanskrit compounds in which this author delights: নব 'new,' তৃণ 'grass,' বিশিষ্ট 'provided with.'

11. দেড়তালা 'one-and-a-half storey (high),' said of a house having the lower storey the full height and another above it only half the full height.

13. ফ্লুটেড্. This is meant for the English word 'fluted.'

16. Another compound: তৃণ 'grass,' পুষ্প 'flower,' ময় termination with general meaning of 'having,' 'possessing.'

16. This is the description of the first block of buildings, consisting of a large open hall or *boiṭakkhānā*, where the master of the house sits to receive his guests or to rest; then his *daftar khāna*, study or writing rooms, and *kāchhāri* or office where his clerks sit and the tenants come to pay their rents and transact business. Next to this is a block of buildings devoted to religious ceremonies, and a third containing temples and idols; connected with the last are rooms for cooking the offerings and food for the priests, also apartments for the reception of religious mendicants who are always wandering about the country.

30. These three blocks constitute the *sadar* or principal part of the house, the public reception rooms, and business part. Behind these are three other blocks, called the *andar* or private part, namely, the owner's own apartments, a large building inhabited by a swarm of female relations, and the cooking department.

42. The perpetual hubbub kept up by the poor relations is here described.

49. Here we have the proceedings of the female cooks vividly described.

VI.

This extract also is in pure classical Bengali, and requires little or no explanation. It is part of a letter supposed to be written by the hero's wife, when he falls in love with and marries a second wife, and the writer, unable to endure his desertion of her, runs away from home, and takes farewell in these few words of her sister-in-law, Kamalmaṇi.

Line 7. Kundanandinī is the second wife. She too had run away, but they found her again.

14. কিন্তু etc. This somewhat involved sentence will be best understood by taking it backwards, beginning at সাধ ছিল 'it was (my) object to go (after) having seen with my own eyes for two or

three days my husband's happiness, that happiness for the sake of which I myself destroyed my own life.'

21. দূর যাইব 'I shall *be* far off;' *be*, not *go*, in our idiom.

23. তুমি আসিতে দিতে না 'you would not have let me *go;*' we should say *go* where the Bengali says *come*.

27. আশীর্বাদ here rather 'a good wish' than strictly 'a blessing.'

VII.

The novel from which this and the following extract are taken appeared some forty years ago, and is thus one of the earliest novels in Bengali. The style is colloquial, and contains very few of the Sanskrit compounds which have become fashionable in later works. The story is one with a moral, and depicts in vivid colours the evil results of over-indulgence of children by their parents. In this extract the father, Bāburām Bābu, has just received the news of his son Matilāl's having been arrested by the police, whereupon he sends for a well-known *mukhtār* or pleader, and takes his advice as to the course to be pursued.

Line 1. টাকাতে অতিশয় মায়া 'was very fond of his money.'

7. সুস্থির হইয়া 'when he had recovered from the shock.'

8. বড় পটু 'very sharp,' implying also that he was not very scrupulous. To understand the full force of this satirical description of a type of lawyer unfortunately still only too frequently met with, it would be necessary to live in Bengal and have business in the law courts.

10. জাল করিতে 'to forge documents.' সাক্ষী সাজাইয়া দিতে 'to tutor witnesses;' this is a most important branch of a *mukhtār's* business.

11. বশ করিতে 'to get into (his) power,' 'to establish an understanding with' the police-officers who investigate criminal cases, and the clerks in the magistrate's office through whose hands the papers of the case pass. A polite synonym for bribery.

14. ঠকচাচা 'Uncle Rogue;' this was his sobriquet, and he was proud of it.

16. রমজান. The fast kept by all pious Muslims, and Uncle Rogue was very pious.

21. মুকদ্দমা উড়াইয়া দিতে 'to cause a case to fly,' i.e. to win it, or, more strictly, to cause the accusation to break down, by bribing or bringing false witnesses.

22. পাকা ২ লোক lit. 'ripe' or 'well-cooked' people, i.e. men who could be relied on to swear to anything they were wanted to.

23. তেনাদের vulgarism for তাহাদের.

24. জিতুব 'I will win.' কেলু, 25. এজু vulgarisms for কালি and আজি respectively.

25. চল্লাম lit. 'I have gone,' i.e. I go—I am off!

VIII.

Here the further misconduct of the spoilt child is related.

Line 3. বুড়া বেটা, a disrespectful way of speaking of his father, 'the old boy.'

4. চোক বুজলে 'having closed his eyes.' The whole sentence means 'when the old boy shuts his eyes I will play the Bābu to my heart's content,' i.e. as soon as his father is dead.

6. বলে বসিত 'he used to say,' lit. 'he used to sit saying.'

9. শিব রাত্রির শলিতা, an allusion to the lamps lighted on the night of the Shiba festival, which it is a great object to keep burning all night in order to obtain a blessing.

10. বেঁচে থাকুক etc. The meaning is that they regarded their son as their only hope, and, so long as he lived, it did not matter what happened to them—a handful of water would suffice for their subsistence. বেঁচে = বাঁচিয়া.

11. বনভোজন. This and the various amusements to which Matilāl was addicted will be found explained in the glossary. They are mostly dancing, singing, acting, and fighting parties of various kinds.

17. সিদ্ধি etc. These are various preparations of opium and hemp, used as narcotics and intoxicants in Bengal.

19. সিপাই পেড়ে 'having a red border or edging,' called 'soldiers' border.'

IX.

The movement associated with the name of Ishwara Chandra led to the almost unrestricted use of Sanskrit words in Bengali. As an example of this style, which, though bombastic and artificial, has become very popular, this and the following extract are given. They consist, it will be seen, almost entirely of Sanskrit words. The subject of the work is the well-worn story of Rāma and Sītā, and in the present passage Rāma describes the charms of the Pampā lake in the Daṇḍaka forest in Central India, which he had seen on a former occasion when searching for Sītā.

X.

In this passage Sītā laments Rāma's cruelty to her, and attributes it to some sins she has committed in a previous state of existence. With the exception of one or two long Sanskrit compounds there is no special difficulty calling for explanation,

Line 9. পতি 'husband,' বিয়োজিতা 'deprived of,' 'separated from.'

13. পূর্ব্ব 'former,' জন্ম 'birth,' অর্জ্জিত 'earned,' 'deserved.' The whole sentence means 'this is only the enjoyment of the fruit of action deserved in a former birth,' which is a little confused in expression, though it is easy to see what the idea is.

XI.

This and the following extracts are from actual official papers on record in a certain district in Bengal, the name of which, together with the names of most of the persons and places mentioned, has been purposely changed. Some of these papers are taken from the Magistrate's office, and refer to criminal matters; others are taken from the Collector's office, and relate to the collection of the revenue and matters incidental thereto. The style of all of them is more or less bad, abounding with grammatical mistakes, awkwardly constructed sentences, misspellings, and foreign words, most of which are incorrectly applied. The very badness of the style, however, has its value, as it is in this style that all the official documents of the country are written. The student, if engaged in any branch of the public service, will find most of the business papers that come before him composed in this style. These extracts also abound in technical terms constantly employed in official business, the knowledge of which will be very useful. This is a case in which a man has had some articles stolen, and comes to the Police Station to make a complaint, and have the matter enquired into.

Heading: দঃ বিঃ stand for দণ্ডবিধি, i.e. দণ্ড 'punishment,' বিধি 'law,' the name by which the Indian Penal Code is known throughout Bengal.

Line 2. ষ্টেশনে the English word 'Station,' meaning the Thānā or Police Station. উপস্থিতে an error for উপস্থিত হইয়া 'being present.' বুধবারের should be বুধবার 'Wednesday.'

3. রাত্রি should be রাত্রে 'at night.'

4. আপন গায়ের 'of my own body,' i.e. a cloth that I used to wear.

7. দুই দণ্ড থাকিতে 'when two daṇḍas remained,' i. e. about an hour before daybreak.

8. শুইয়া থাকা an incorrect expression; it should be শুইয়াছিল যে 'who had been sleeping.'

12. এতক is more a Hindustani than a Bengali expression; it would be better expressed by আজ পর্য্যন্ত, এপর্য্যন্ত, or এতেক.

18. কান্ ফিতা a sort of narrow tape used for binding the edges of clothes.

19. The weight of the pot is given in figures and words as 'one ser,' or 'one-and-a-quarter ser,' and the value further on in figures as 'eight anas.'

XII.

In this case also there is a complaint of theft.

Heading: ধারা means a section of the Code. The present case is put under secs. 379 and 411. মোঃ stands for মোকদ্দম 'a case.'

Line 4. রাইটার কনষ্টেবল the English words 'writer constable.' Official documents are full of English words spelt phonetically.

7. গত etc. This is a good specimen of the way in which the words in a sentence are arranged in the opposite order to English. It runs thus: 'the day before yesterday my uncle G. N. Ghose (to) Goāsi on going he having taken had gone, in mind I made.' What he means is that he missed the coat and shirt, and thought his uncle had taken them.

10. লইয়া যান নাই present indefinite used in a past sense, 'the uncle said he did not take, or had not taken, them.'

15. আসিতে থাকায় should be আসায়.

16. চুরি যাওয়া bad grammar; it should be চুরি গয়াছিল যে. ধরি present used for past again, 'I seized (him).'

22. মোকদ্দমা etc. These words down to পিরানটি are a speech; the complainant says to Kāki Shekh, 'I will not make a complaint against you, brother, give me my shirt,' whereupon Kāki produced the shirt, and complainant *did* make a complaint!

34. চিনিবেক erroneous for চিনিবেন 'they will identify.'

XIII.

Line 2. হাং short for হাল 'at present.'

3. পঞ্চাইতের এতেলা 'information or report from the pañchāyat.' Their duty is to report the occurrence of any crime in their village; they therefore sent the report by the village watchman or *chaukidār*.

6. নামান শব্দ wrongly for নামাওযার 'noise of bringing down.'

13. মাল আদি 'property etc.'

14. নিম্নের মাল 'the under-mentioned property;' there is usually a list of the property stolen appended to the complaint.

17. নামান বাক্সে, this phrase, though not uncommon, is incorrect; it should be নামাইয়াছিল যে বক্স.

18. পাহারা, a striking instance of the Bengali habit of lengthening the vowels of foreign words. This is a Hindustani word, and is properly পহরা, under which spelling it will be found in the glossary. গেলে, correctly গেলে পর 'after he had gone.'

XIV.

In this petition the *chaukidār* complains to the Magistrate that he has been dismissed from his post, though he has done nothing wrong, merely because his brother had once been imprisoned for theft some years ago. He prays to be re-instated.

Line 8. দুষ্কর্ম্মের কার্য্য is a pleonasm, 'an act of bad action!' the first word alone would have sufficed.

11. ডিঃ সুঃ stand for 'District Superintendent,' the chief officer of police in a district.

12. আমি . . . পারিয়া. Inverted sentence, as usual in Bengali. It means 'having been able to know (i. e. having ascertained) (*that*) I (was) the brother of, etc.'

13. আমাকে . . . করিয়া. Similar construction to the above:

'having judged (that) it is not good to keep me appointed (i.e. to retain me) in the work of chaukidār.'

15. সব ইঃ stand for 'Sub-Inspector,' the officer in charge of a police station. This sentence also is rather involved, and must be read backwards: 'he orders (ordered) the Sub-Inspector of the Morkhālī Thānā to give a report with (containing) a request of dismissing me.'

20. চাকরিটি ছিল বলিয়া 'having said, there was service,' i.e. relying upon or depending upon his appointment, he managed somehow to exist. রূপ is quite superfluous here, and টা is wrongly written for টি.

24. স্বত্বে ও 'even in being,' i.e. in spite of the fact that.

XV.

The petitioner in this case also has been dismissed, and prays to be re-instated.

Line 3. ছোট বেলা হইতে 'from an early age.'

6. দিয়াছিলেন 'they gave;' with বদলী it means 'they transferred,' i.e. the authorities.

12. কর্জ্জ পত্র 'debt and writing,' meaning a loan secured by a bond.

16. বুড়াম শেখ a man's name. The structure of this sentence is somewhat irregular. He means that he seized a thief who had been committing a theft at the house of the persons named.

21. ফেলসামি, an attempt at writing the Arabic words فعل شنيع 'criminal action,' the technical term in Indian law for adultery.

32. চাপরাস (also written চাপ্রাশ), a brass badge, with an inscription on it, worn at the belt by village watchmen, messengers, and others. He asks to have his *chāprās* given back to him, i.e. to be restored to his post.

XVI.

An objection made by certain persons to the registration of the names of certain other persons in the Collector's register as part proprietors of an estate. This is a very common legal proceeding, the full explanation of which cannot of course be given in this place.

Line 2. নাম জারি, two Persian words meaning 'name current,' technically applied to having one's name recorded as a proprietor in the Collector's books.

4. স্বত্বাধিকার, here the writer has mixed up two words into a long compound, স্বত্ব 'right' and অধিকার 'authority.'

6. খাজানাদি, here the Sanskrit word আদি 'etc.' has been strangely tacked on to the Arabic word خزانه 'revenue.' এমতাবস্থায়, again, has two words run into one, এমত 'such' and অবস্থা 'circumstance.'

10. প্রকৃত প্রস্তাবে 'in simple mention,' i.e. the plain facts of the case are these.

14. কালেক্টরীর, the English word 'Collector' with the Bengali termination ঈ to it, meaning the Collectorate or Collector's office.

15. বরাত, a cheque or order for payment. The proprietress drew a cheque, or wrote an order for payment of the revenue, on the patnīdār or subordinate tenure holder to whom she had leased a portion of the estate.

16. দখলীকারিণী, a characteristic instance of the confusion of forms that exists in official language. The Sanskrit feminine termination ইণী is added to the Persian word *dakhalkār* to express the idea of 'proprietress,' and a superfluous ī or ĭ is inserted. থাকনাবস্থায়, two words rolled into one, থাকন 'remaining' and অবস্থা.

23. বিনামদার. It is a common practice in India for persons

to buy estates and transact business not in their own name, but in that of some relation or dependant. Such transactions are called benāmī or 'without name.' The benāmdār (here corruptly written bĭnām) is the tool who lends his name, but has no interest or right in the property.

XVII.

Reasons why a certain estate should not be divided into separate shares among the joint proprietors, as desired by them. It is here alleged that the proprietors had already effected a partition privately among themselves, which, if true, would be a legal bar to a partition being made by the Collector.

Line 3. স্বীকারানুসারে, two words joined together, স্বীকার 'admission,' 'consent,' অনুসারে 'according to.'

4. আপোষে, an altogether erroneous method of writing the Hindustani word آپس *āpas*, which has found its way into Bengali. It means here 'among themselves.'

5. তদবধি, two words joined together, তদ 'that,' অবধি 'limit,' 'period;' the whole compound means 'since then.'

10. ৷৵. অংশ, a six-anas share. An estate (and most other visible or conceivable objects) is considered to be divisible, like a rupee, into sixteen parts. Thus $\frac{6}{16}$ of an estate is a six-anas share. So in line 12, ৷৷৵. a ten-anas share or $\frac{5}{8}$ of the estate. The petition recites that the proprietors of the six- and ten-anas shares have taken possession of their respective shares, and made them into new and separate estates, which is expressed by ষোল আনা রকম or a sixteen-ana fraction.

18. ছায়, probably a slip of the pen for ছাড়া 'except.'

19. আইনানুসারে, compound again; this time অনুসারে 'according to' is tacked on to the Persian word آئین ā-īn, 'law!'

XVIII.

A brief petition setting forth that the petitioner, and not Messrs. Roberts & Co., is the proper person to take the settlement of an estate.

Line 2. সেবাইতী, pertaining to a Sebait or person who worships an idol. Here the meaning is that (theoretically and ostensibly) the estate is one the rents of which are appropriated to the maintenance of a Hindu temple and the services thereof.

6. হাই কোর্ট the 'High Court' of Judicature at Calcutta.

9. নিলাম খরিদার রূপে 'in the capacity of auction purchasers.'

10. সাহেবান, the Persian plural صاحبان 'sāhibs,' 'gentlemen.'

XIX.

The case here is similar to that in extract XVI.

Line 8. তৎস্থলে 'in place of him,' i.e. of Āshutosh.

14. অবস্থানুসারে, the first part is অবস্থা 'condition,' 'circumstance;' here 'the facts of the case.'

16. হয়েন for হন 'are' not. তন্মূলে 'on that ground,' 'for that reason.'

XX.

This rather old-fashioned document is a good specimen of what the student, if in the service of Government, will often come across in settlement work. It is a rambling, pompous proceeding, which recites at great length a number of previous transactions. It is full of misspelt and misapplied Persian words, the knowledge of which is essential in official life. The preamble contains only one genuine Bengali word. The Arabic and Persian words will be found in the glossary.

Line 10. ইত্যগ্রে, compound, ইতি 'thus,' অগ্রে 'before;' the whole meaning 'heretofore.'

11. কানুনগো from Persian قانون گو 'law-teller,' formerly an officer whose duty it was to keep a record of all customary rights and unwritten laws relating to the tenure of land. In Bengal, in the present day, they are employed chiefly in surveying and assessing estates for revenue purposes.

14. পয়বাস্ত, a corruption of a Persian word meaning 'joined.' Owing to a change in the course of the Khariyā river, a sandbank had been formed contiguous to the village of Durlabhpūr, and the measurement and assessment to revenue of this sandbank, called a 'char,' is the subject of this extract.

18. প্রতিবাদীত্ব, an absurd addition of the affix ত্ব to the word প্রতিবাদী 'defendant,' thus making a word 'defendantship!'

25. খাস কমিসনর, the Special Commissioners appointed for the trial of cases of this kind.

30. কুইনকুইনিয়াল, the English word 'quinquennial,' i.e. a register of estates which in former times used to be kept up, and re-written every five years, whence its name.

34. কর ধার্য 'assessment of revenue.' The land having been declared not to be included in any revenue-paying estate, the suit brought by Government to declare it liable to payment of revenue was decreed in their favour, and permission given to make an assessment of revenue on it.

GLOSSARY

TO THE

SPECIMENS OF BENGALI LITERATURE.

অ

অংশ *s.* a share, part.

অগ্নি *s.* fire.

অগ্রে *ad.* before, formerly, previously.

অজুহাৎ *s.* (corrupted from Pers. وجوهات, irregular formation from Ar. وجوه plural of وَجْه a cause, reason) arguments, reasons.

অতি *prep.* very, excessively.

অতিথি *s.* a guest, applied generally to religious mendicants.

অতিথিশালা *s.* a house for lodging strangers, guest-house.

অতিশয় *a.* excessive; *ad.* excessively, extremely.

অতীত *a.* past, elapsed, gone by.

অত্যন্ত *ad.* very, very much, excessively.

অত্র *ad.* here, this, herein-mentioned.

অথবা *conj.* or, otherwise.

অদ্য *ad.* to-day.

অধিক *a.* more, more than.

অধিকার *s.* right, authority, power; the legal right to do anything.

অধিকারী *a.* one who possesses a right; ruler; proprietor.

অধীন *a.* subject to, subordinate; (in addressing superiors) your humble servant.

অনন্তর *a.* succeeding, (lit. without an interval, hence) continuous, incessant; *ad.* immediately after, afterwards.

অনবরত *a.* incessant, perpetual, in unbroken succession.

অনর্থক *a.* unmeaning, useless, vain.

অনির্বচনীয় *a.* unspeakable, indescribable.

অনুক্ষণ *ad.* at every moment, continually, incessantly.

অনুচ্চ *a.* low, not lofty; humble, mean.

অনুমতি *s.* permission, sanction.

অনুযায়ী *a.* pursuant to, in consequence of, in accordance with.

অনুসারে *ad.* according to.

অনেক *a.* some, many.

অন্তঃকরণ *s.* the heart, mind; the inner man.

অন্তর *s.* the midst, the inside of a thing; interval, distance.

অন্তরে *ad.* inside, within.

অন্দর *s.* (Pers. اندر) the interior or private apartments; the female apartments.

অন্ধ *a.* blind.

অন্ধকার *s.* darkness.

অন্ধার *s.* (popular form of above) darkness.

অন্য *a.* other, different.

অন্যান্য *a.* other, various, several.

অন্বেষণ *s.* enquiry, search.

অপযশ *s.* disgrace, bad name.

অপরাধ *s.* offence, crime.

অপরিমিত *a.* immeasurable, unlimited.

অপরিষ্কৃত *a.* not kept clean, not purified.

অপেক্ষা *s.* expectation; *ad.* in comparison, than, rather.

অবকাশ *s.* leisure, opportunity.

অবলোকন *s.* looking at, regarding.

অবশিষ্ট *a.* remaining, other, left over.

অবশ্য *a.* certain, necessary; *ad.* certainly, of course, undoubtedly.

অবস্থা *s.* state, condition.

অবাক *a.* speechless, mute, mute from wonder, astonished.

অভদ্র *a.* bad, unfavourable, improper.

অভিপ্রায় *s.* object, intention, design.

অ্যাও *pron.* (vulgar) this, for ইহাও.

অ্যাত *pron.* (vulgar) so much, for এত.

অর্থাৎ *ad.* i.e., that is to say.

অসৎ *a.* wicked, evil.

অসুবিধ *a.* uneasy, inconvenient, unsuitable.

অস্ত্র *s.* weapon, missile, arms.

অহঙ্কার *s.* selfishness, egotism, pride.

আ

আইন *s.* (Pers. آئین) a law, rule.

আকড়া *s.* (more correctly আখড়া) a wrestling match, an assembly for singing, wrestling, fencing, dancing, etc.

আকার *s.* form, figure, appearance.

আছে *v.* is (the defective subst. verb).

আজ *ad.* to-day.

আজা *s.* (corruption of রাজা) king. আজদূত (corruption of রাজদূত) king's messenger, herald.

আজ্ঞা *s.* command, order; *ad.* yes (to a superior).

আজলা *s.* a bag or wallet carried by religious mendicants (also written আঁচলা).

আঞ্জাম *s.* (Pers. انجام) end, termination, the completion of an affair.

আড়ে *ad.* cross-wise, across.

আতর *s.* (Ar. عطر) attar of roses.

আত্মীয় *a.* belonging to oneself, one's own.

আদর *s.* respect, esteem, veneration.

আদায় *s.* (Ar. ادا, corruptly also ادای) payment, the act of paying.

আদালত *s.* (Ar. عدالت) lit. justice; a court of justice.

আদি *a.* initial; *s.* the first in a series. Principally used to express 'et caetera,' &c.

আদেশ *s.* a command, an instruction, injunction (less forcible than আজ্ঞা).

আদৌ *ad.* (the locative case of আদি lit. 'in the beginning') generally used with a negative to imply 'not at all,' 'never under any circumstances,' 'void *ab initio*.'

আনন্দ *s.* joy.

আনা *s.* an *ānā*, the sixteenth part of a rupee.

আন্দাজ *s.* (Pers. انداز lit. 'throwing') a guess, conjecture; an approximate estimate. Often used adverbially for 'about,' 'more or less.'

আন্দোলিত *a.* swung, shaken.

আপত্তি *s.* objection, remonstrance, legal obstacle.

আপত্তিকারী *s.* objector.

আপন *a.* own (also আপনা).

আপনি *pron.* self.

আপসে *pron.* (corruptly written আপোষে) among (our-, your-, them-) selves, mutually.

আপীল *s.* (English word) appeal.

আবার *ad.* again.

আবেদন *s.* a representation, respectful statement of facts.

আমলে *s.* (Ar. أمل business) effect, (with আস্) to take effect, to be effected.

আমীন *s.* (Ar. أمين) a person appointed to measure land, an *Amīn.*

আমোদিত *a.* gratified, pleased.

আম্লা *s.* (more correctly অম্লা, Ar. عمل plural of عامل a doer, manager) a collective term for all the clerks in an office, or for the profession of clerks in general; clerks, writers, petty officials. Their official designation in India is 'ministerial officers.'

আয়, আয়ঃ or **আয়স্** *s.* life.

আর *conj.* and.

আরাজী *s.* (Ar. أراضى pl. of أرض land) lands, landed property.

আরাজীয়াৎ same as the above with the addition of a redundant plural termination *-yāt*, often added corruptly to Arabic words.

আরে *interj.* Ho! Hullo! a contemptuous form of address.

আর্য *a.* noble, honourable, (as a form of address) Noble Sir!

আর্যপুত্র *s.* son of a noble, a respectful term used by a wife when speaking to or of her husband (high literary style).

আলগা *a.* unconnected, separate.

আলিশা *s.* the cornice on the top of a house.

আলো *s.* a light, flame.

আশা *s.* hope.

আশীর্বাদ *s.* a benediction, a blessing at parting.

আশ্চর্য *a.* wonderful, astonishing.

আসক্ত *a.* attached to, addicted to, fond of.

আসবাব *s.* (Ar. أسباب pl. of سَبَب a cause; compare Latin *causa* and Italian *cosa*, 'a thing') goods and chattels, furniture, stores, luggage, materials.

আসামী *s.* (Ar. اسامى corrupt formation from إسم a name) named, the person named in legal proceedings, a defendant, accused, criminal.

আহা *interj.* alas!

আহার *s.* food.

ই

ইংরাজী *a.* English.

ইচ্ছা *s.* will, wish.

ইতি *ad.* thus, (in comp.) the present time.

ইতিপূর্ব্বে *ad.* before this, heretofore, formerly.

ইতিমধ্যে *ad.* meanwhile, in the meantime, during this.

ইন্দুর *s.* a rat.

ইন্‌স্পেক্‌টর *s.* (the English word) Inspector.

ঈ

ঈদ *s.* (Ar. عيد) a festival. The name of two Musulman festivals: 1. the *īdu'l fiṭr* or 'festival of breaking the fast,' held at the close of the fast of Ramzān; 2. the *īdu'lazḥa'* or 'festival of the victims,' held on the tenth of the month Zu'l Hijja in commemoration of Abraham's sacrifice of Ishmael (*not* Isaac) as the Musulmans say.

ঈষৎ *ad.* slightly, a little, some.

উ

উক্ত *a.* said, mentioned, the aforesaid.

উচিত *a.* proper, fit, suitable, convenient.

উচ্চ *a.* high, lofty.

উজু *s.* (Ar. وضو) the ablutions performed by Musulmans before prayers.

উঠ্ *v.* to rise, get up.

উঠান *s.* a raised platform, paved courtyard, enclosure.

উড়্ *v. act.* to fly.

উড়া *v. caus.* to cause to fly, to throw up into the air, to get rid of.

উত্তর *s.* subsequent, posterior, succeeding; north.

উত্তরাধিকারী *s.* heir, successor.

উত্তাপ *s.* heat, ardour, distress.

উদর *s.* belly.

উদ্যোগী *a.* active, industrious, strenuous in exertion.

উন্নত *a.* increased, exalted, prosperous.

উন্মত্ত *a.* intoxicated, mad; raving.

উন্মাদ *s.* intoxication.

উপযুক্ত *a.* fitted, suited for.

উপরি *prep.* above, upon, over.

উপস্থিত *a.* standing by, present, in attendance.

উপায় *s.* an expedient, remedy, means of accomplishing.

উভয় *pron.* both.

উল্লিখিত *a.* written out, described, re[illegible] a document).

এ

এক *num.* one.

একাকী *a.* alone, solitary.

একান্ত *a.* sole, entire, absolute; *ad.* solely, entirely.

এক্‌লাই *a.* having a single border (a shirt).

এখন *ad.* now.

এজ *ad.* (corruption of আজ) to-day.

এজহার *s.* (Ar. اظهار making clear) a deposition, statement, evidence of a witness in a case. (Sometimes corruptly written এজাহার.)

এত *pron.* so much.

এতক *ad.* (corrupt or vulgar expression) up to the present time, till now.

এত্তেলা *s.* (Ar. اطلاع) information, cognizance, news.

এবং *conj.* and, also.

এমন *a.* thus, in this manner, of this kind.

এমনে *ad. id.*

ও

ও *conj.* and, also.

ওড়া *pron.* (corrupted for ওটা) that.

ওহ্‌দা *s.* (Ar. عهده) post, appointment, office.

ক

ক *pron.* (properly কঃ) who? which?

কই *ad.* (also written কৈ) where?

কখন *ad.* when? at any time. কখনও or কখনো sometimes, (with a negative) never. কখন . . . . কখন at one time . . . . at another.

কচুরী *s.* a kind of sweet cake.

কচ্‌কচি *s.* murmuring, grumbling.

কণ্ঠরোধ *s.* stopping of the throat, a choking sensation (from grief).

কত *pron.* how much? how many?

কথা *s.* story, speech, statement of any matter.

কথিত *a.* told, said, expressed.

কন্যা *s.* a virgin, maiden, bride.

কপাল *s.* the forehead; destiny, fate. (The idea is that a man's destiny is written invisibly on his forehead at birth.)

কবি *s.* a poet. কবিওয়ালা a singer.

কমণ্ডলু *s.* a kind of waterpot used by fakirs.

কমল *s.* a lotus.

কয়েদ *s.* (Ar. قيد bond, fetter) imprisonment. কয়েদ করিতে to put in prison.

কর্ *v.* to do, make.

কর *s.* the hand; a tax.

কর্জ *s.* (Ar. قرض loan) debt, indebtedness.

কর্ত্তা *s.* a doer, agent; master, governor.

কর্ম্ম *s.* deed, action.

কলকল *s.* a babbling, brawling, chattering noise.

কলহ *s.* quarrel, strife, dispute.

কল্য *ad.* to-morrow; yesterday.

কষ্ট *s.* trouble, pain, distress.

কসে *ad.* with effort, ardently, earnestly.

কস্মিন্ কালে (two Sanskrit words) at what time? at any time, (with negative) never.

কাংসা *s.* bell-metal, a mixture of zinc and copper.

কাঁচা *a.* unripe, uncooked; imperfect, defective.

কাঁদাকাটী *s.* weeping, lamentation.

কাক *s.* a crow.

কাকা *s.* a father's younger brother, paternal uncle.

কাকী *s.* father's younger brother's wife.

কাগজ *s.* (Pers. کاغذ) paper.

কাছারী *s.* a public office, court of justice, (vulgo) cutcherry.

কাছী *s.* string.

কাছে *prep.* near, by the side of, close to; in the possession of.

কাজ *s.* work, business, affair.

কাজে *ad.* because of, therefore, on that account.

কাট্ *v. act.* to cut (used in all the senses of the English word).

কাটা *v. caus.* to cause to cut; *s.* a measure of land, also of capacity, a bushel or peck.

কাটি *s.* a small stick.

কাঠ *s.* wood.

কাণ *s.* the ear.

কাৎ *s.* full value, full measure, sufficiency.

কাতর *a.* distressed, troubled.

কাপড় *s.* cloth, esp. cotton cloth; clothes in general.

কামনা *s.* wish, desire.

কামিনী *s.* a young woman.

কারণ *s.* cause.

কার্য্য *s.* business, duty, work.

কালি *ad.* to-morrow, yesterday.

কাশ্মীরী *a.* belonging to Cashmere (Kāshmīr), Cashmere cloth or shawl.

কি } what?
কিং }

কিছু *pron.* anything, something. কিছু মাত্র (with negative) nothing at all, not the least.

কিন্ *v. act.* to buy.

কিন্তু *conj.* but.

কিম্বা *conj.* or.

কিয়ৎ *pron.* some, a few, little.

কুটুম্ব *s.* family, relationship; a relation.

কুটুম্বিনী *s.* a female relation.

কুঠরী, কুঠারী *s.* a room.

কুঠার *s.* an axe, hatchet.

কুড়া *s.* a bigha of land.

কুতর্ক *s.* mistake, error of judgment.

কুদ্রৎ *s.* (Ar. قدرت) power, force, ability.

কুনির্মিত *s.* badly built.

কুসংসর্গ *s.* bad society, bad company.

কৃতাঞ্জলী *a.* with hands joined (in prayer). কৃতাঞ্জলী পূর্বক *ad.* most humbly and respectfully.

কৃপণ *s.* a miser.

কেতা *s.* (Ar. قطعه a piece) a piece, a word put before letters or papers.

কেন *ad.* why? কেন না because.

কেবল *ad.* only.

কেমন *ad.* how?

কেলি *s.* sport, play.

কেশ *s.* hair.

কোট *s.* (the English word) a coat.

কোঠা *s.* a room, house.

কোণ *s.* a corner.

কোথা *ad.* where?

কোন *pron.* any one. কোন্ who?

কোমল *a.* tender, soft, delicate.

ক্রম *s.* a step. ক্রমে *ad.* by degrees, gradually.

ক্রমান্বিত *a.* consecutive, following one another.

ক্রয় *s.* purchase, buying.

ক্ষণ *s.* a minute, an instant of time.

ক্ষণেক্ *ad.* for an instant, for a single moment (only).

ক্ষুদ্র *a.* small, little.

খ

খণ্ড *s.* a piece, part, division of land or other things.

খরীদ *s.* (Pers. خريد) purchase.

খরীদার *s.* (Pers. خريدار) purchaser.

খর্চ, খরচ *s.* expenditure, cost.

খলাসী *s.* a soldier, sailor, (vulgo) an outdoor servant, tent pitcher, etc.

খলিফা *s.* (Ar. خليفه successor of the prophet 'Caliph') a term commonly applied to tailors in India.

খা *v.* to eat.

খাওয়া *v. caus.* to cause to eat, to feed.

খাজনা *s.* (corrupted from Ar. خزانه treasure) rent of land, revenue of estates.

খানাখা *ad.* (Pers. خواه نخواه willing or not willing) unexpectedly, without rhyme or reason, capriciously.

খালী *a.* (Ar. خالي) empty, vacant.

খাস *a.* (Ar. خاص) excellent, peculiar, private; (in Indian revenue language) estates held direct by Government.

খাসা গোজা *s.* a kind of sweetmeat.

খাজা *s.* a kind of sweetmeat.

খিলি *s.* a packet, a small triangular package of betel-nut and spices wrapped in a pān-leaf, used for chewing.

খুড়া *s.* father's younger brother.

খুল্ *v.* to open.

খুব *a.* (Pers. خوب) beautiful, excellent; (vulgo) much, very.

খেমটা *s.* a class of dancing-girls from the north-western provinces.

খোলা *a.* open, (a hut) having walls on three sides only.

গ

গজা *v.* to sprout, shoot up.

গণ্ডা *s.* an aggregate of four; in the old sikkā coinage twenty gaṇḍās made one anna.

গণ্ডুষ *s.* a handful of water, (met.) a bare livelihood.

গণ্য *a.* that may be counted, calculable, appreciable.

গত *a.* past, gone. গত কালি yesterday.

গতিক *s.* state, condition; progress, course of events.

গমন *s.* going, walking.

গরিব *a.* (Ar. غريب) poor, humble; (also, and better, written গরীব.)

গল্ *v.* to dissolve, melt; to escape; to overflow with pride, joy, etc.

গলা *s.* the neck.

গল্প *s.* talk, gossip, babble, chattering.

গাঁজা *s.* the dried flowers and leaves of hemp smoked as a narcotic and intoxicant; *gānjā.*

গাঁত *s.* a neighbour, acquaintance.

গাছ *s.* a tree.

গাজ *s.* (the English word) gauze.

গান *s.* singing, song.

গায় *s.* the body, and গায়ে *ad.* on the body, wrapped round one, (said of garments) গায় দিতে to put on, wear.

গুজর *s.* (Pers. گذر crossing) the crossing over a river.

গুজরান *s.* (Pers. گذران) passing, spending (time); living, subsisting.

গুড়ুক *s.* tobacco mixed with molasses, for smoking.

গুন *s.* buzzing, humming.

গুলি *s.* a pill (of opium or other drug).

গৃহ *s.* a house.

গেলাস *s.* (the English word) a glass, a brass or metal cup made in the shape of a tumbler.

গো *s.* a cow; a method of addressing relations in the colloquial style.

গোট *s.* rolling up, gathering up.

গোমস্তা *s.* (Pers. گماشته part. pass. commissioned, entrusted) an agent, steward, manager.

গোলাবী *s.* mixed with, or scented with, rosewater.

গোলা *s.* a ball, round mass.

গ্রস্ত *a.* seized, swallowed.

গ্রহণ *s.* taking, seizing; an eclipse.

গ্রাম *s.* a village.

ঘ

ঘট্ *v.* to occur, happen.

ঘটনা *s.* an occurrence, event, incident.

ঘটা *v. caus.* to cause to occur; *s.* a crowd, concourse of people.

ঘর *s.* a house; a native place or ancestral home as distinguished from a temporary residence.

ঘাট *s.* a landing-place, steps leading down to a river; place where a river is crossed, a ferry.

ঘাস *s.* grass.

ঘুচা *v.* to open, dispel (doubt), remove.

ঘুম্ *v.* to sleep.

ঘুম *s.* sleep.

ঘৃণা *s.* hatred, disgust, dislike.

চ

চক্ *s.* a square, courtyard, market-place.

চক্ষু *s.* the eye.

চতুর্দশ *a.* fourteen, the fourteenth.

চতুর্দিকে *ad.* on all sides.

চতুষ্পার্শ্বে *ad.* on all sides.

চত্বর *s.* a courtyard.

চপ্রাস *s.* a brass badge worn by certain classes of public servants, such as policemen, village watchmen, office messengers, etc.

চর *s.* a sandbank in a river.

চরস *s.* an intoxicating drug made from hemp.

চরিত্র *s.* mental disposition, character, conduct.

চল্ *v.* to go, move, pass.

চা *v.* to wish, ask for; to look at. (Also **চাহ্**.)

চাঁপা *s.* the flower of the champā tree, a silver jewel made in the shape of a champā flower.

চাকরী *s.* service, employment.

চাবী *s.* a key.

চারি *a.* four.

চালি *s.* rice.

চাষা *s.* a ploughman, cultivator, peasant.

চিক *s.* an ornament of gold or silver worn round the neck.

চিন্ *v.* to recognise, identify.

চির *a.* long (of time). **চিরসুখী** happy for ever.

চীৎকার *s.* noise, disturbance.

চূড়া *s.* topknot, lock of hair.

চুরি *s.* theft.

চুল *s.* a lock of hair, the hair of the head.

চেঁচা *v.* to bawl, scream, rave.

চোক *s.* (vulgar) eye.

চোর *s.* thief.

চৌকীদার *s.* a village watchman.

ছ

ছড়ি *s.* a walking-stick.

ছাএল *s.* (Ar. سایل asker) a petitioner.

ছাড়্ *v.* to leave, abandon; to let go, release.

ছাতী *s.* bosom, breast.

ছার *s.* ashes; anything vile, contemptible, unimportant.

ছিট *s.* chintz.

ছিট্কা *v.* to splash, sputter, boil over.

ছেঁড়্ *v. act.* to tear; *v. neut.* to be torn.

ছেলা *s.* a boy, child.

ছোট *a.* small, little, younger (of brothers).

ছোটা *v.* to set free, let loose.

জ

জগদীশ্বর *s.* God, the Lord of the world.

জটা *s.* matted hair, (of a lion) mane.

জন *s.* a man, person.

জন্ম (also written **জনম**) *s.* birth.

জন্মান্তর *s.* another birth, a previous state of existence.

জন্য, জন্যে *ad.* on account of, because of, for.

জবানবন্দী *s.* (Pers. زبان بندی) a written deposition, or evidence.

জমী *s.* (Pers. زمین) land.

জমীদার *s.* (Pers. زمیندار) a landholder, (in revenue language) the person who has engaged with Government for the payment of the revenue of an estate, a Zemindar.

জরী *s.* gold thread, gold embroidery.

জরীপ *s.* (corrupted from Ar. جریب) the measuring of land.

জল *s.* water.

জলকর *s.* a property consisting of the right to catch fish in certain rivers or waters.

জাঁক *s.* a crowd, esp. a noisy crowd.

জান্ *v.* to know.

জায়গা *s.* (corrupted from Pers. جگہ) a place.

জারী *s.* (Ar. جاری flowing) current, in force. **জারী করিতে** to issue (an order).

জাল *s.* a net; (Ar. جعل making) forgery.

জিজ্ঞাসা *s.* a question, asking, enquiry.

জিত্ *v.* to conquer, win (a case).

জিহ্বা *s.* the tongue.

জীব *s.* life.

জুতা *s.* a shoe.

জেলা *s.* (Ar. ضلع) a district.

জোটপাট *s.* machination, falsely got-up case or plot.

জ্ঞানী *s.* wise, intelligent, knowing.

জ্বালা *v.* to light, set fire to, kindle.

ঝ

ঝকঝকী *s.* quarrelling, wrangling.

ঝাঁকড়া *s.* thick curling hair.

ট

টাকা *s.* a rupee.

টালি *s.* (prob. the English word) a tile.

ঠ

ঠাকুর *s.* a god; a respectful method of address to Brahmans etc.

ঠাকুরবাড়ী *s.* a temple.

ঠিক *a.* exact, correct, accurate, just.

ড

ডর *s.* fear.

ডাক্ *v.* to call.

ডাক্ *s.* a shout, call; the post (for letters).

ডাকাডাকী *s.* shouting and calling.

ডাল *s.* the branch of a tree; a kind of grain—split pease.

ডিগ্রী *s.* (the English word) decree; better written **ডিক্রী**.

ডিস্মিস্ *s.* (the English word) dismiss.

ত

তক *ad.* (Hind. تک) until.

তখন *ad.* then.

তথাপি *ad.* although, nevertheless.

তথায় *ad.* there.

তদন্ত *s.* an enquiry, investigation.

তদবধি *ad.* up to that, as far as that, up to that time.

তদ্বিষয় *ad.* in respect to that, concerning that.

তন্মধ্যে *ad.* in the meantime, in the interim.

তন্মূলে *ad.* by reason of that, caused by that.

তপ্ত *a.* heated.

তলব *s.* (Ar. طلب demand) pay, salary, wages; summoning, demanding.

তল্লাস *s.* (corruptly for **তলাস**, Ar. تلاش) search.

তা *pron.* for **তাহা** him, that.

তাজ *s.* (Pers. تاج crown) a high-crowned cap.

তাড়াতাড়ী *ad.* scufflingly, hastily.

তাপ *s.* heat, warmth, distress.

তাবীজ *s.* (Ar. تعويذ seeking protection) an amulet, charm.

তারীখ *s.* (Ar. تاريخ) date of the year, or month, principally of the latter, as **বার তারীখ পৌষ** the 12th of Paush.

তালা *s.* a lock, padlock; the storey of a house.

তিন *a.* three.

তিনি *pron.* he; she.

তিলার্দ্ধ *s.* half (**অর্দ্ধ**) of a til, which is a very small portion of time; i. e. half a second.

তীর *s.* the bank of a river.

তুল্য *a.* equal to, like, similar.

তৃণ *s.* grass. তৃণশূন্য kept clear of grass. তৃণপুষ্পময় adorned with grass and flowers.

তেষ্টা *s.* (corrupted from তৃষ্ণা) thirst.

তোষাখানা *s.* (Pers. توشه‌خانه) a storehouse.

তৈল *s.* oil.

তৈলাক্ত *s.* anointed with oil.

তৌজীহ *s.* (Ar. توجیه or توضیع) the rent-roll of estates kept in the office of the Collector of a district.

ত্যাগ *s.* desertion, abandonment.

থ

থাক্ *v.* to stop, stay.

থানা *s.* a police station.

থাম *s.* a pillar.

দ

দক্ষিণ *a.* south; right hand.

দখল *s.* (Ar. دخل entering) possession.

দখলীকার *s.* in possession, possessing.

দড়ী *s.* rope.

দণ্ড *s.* punishment. দণ্ড বিধি আইন the Penal Code.

দফ্তর্ খানা *s.* (Pers. دفتر خانه) an office room; a study; a counting-house. Also erroneously spelt দপ্তর.

দয়া *s.* pity, mercy.

দরখাস্ত *s.* (Pers. درخواست) a petition, request, application.

দরদালান *s.* an inner hall (see দালান).

দরুন্ *ad.* (Pers. درون within) in, according to, included in.

দল *s.* a body of men, troop, company.

দশনাবলি *s.* a row of teeth.

দাঁত *s.* tooth.

দাখিল *a.* (Ar. داخل entering) filing or putting in information or papers in a case.

দাগ *s.* (Pers. داغ stain, mark) a survey mark, boundary mark.

দাঙ্গা *s.* uproar, affray.

দাদা *s.* elder brother.

দান *s.* gift.

দাবী *s.* (Ar. دعوى) a claim, suit.

দাম *s.* price, cost.

দায় *s.* difficulty, trouble.

দারোগা *s.* (Pers. from Turkish داروغه) an inspector of police, superintendent of a jail or other public office, a *dārogha*.

দালান *s.* a hall, generally open on one side to a courtyard.

দাস *s.* a slave, servant.

দাসী *s.* a female slave, maid-servant.

দিক *s.* trouble, annoyance; a point of the compass.

দিন *s.* day.

দিবস *s.* day.

দীর্ঘ *a.* long. দীর্ঘজীবী long-lived.

দুআনী *s.* a two-anna piece.

দুই *a.* two.

দুঃখ *s.* grief, sorrow, distress.

দুঃখী *a.* sorrowful, distressed.

দুধ *s.* milk.

দুরবস্থা *s.* adversity, distress.

দুরভিসন্ধি *s.* wicked plotting, machination.

দুর্গোৎসব *s.* the annual festival of Durgā; the 'Durgā Pujā.'

দুর্বাক্য *s.* bad language, abuse.

দুষ্কর্ম *s.* evil deed, crime.

দুষ্ট *a.* wicked.

দূর *a.* far, distant; *s.* distance.

দৃষ্ট *a.* seen.

দৃষ্টি *s.* sight, vision, view.

দে *v.* to give (inf. দেওন).

দেওয়া *s.* singing in tune.

দেখ *v.* to see.

দেড় *a.* one-and-a-half.

দেবতা *s.* a deity, god.

দেবমন্দির *s.* a temple.

দেয় *a.* that which must be given, due.

দেরী *s.* lateness, delay.

দেশ *s.* a country, native land.

দেহ *s.* the body.

দৈবাধীন *a.* subject to fate; *ad.* accidentally, as it happened.

দোষ *s.* a fault, offence, crime.

দোষী *a.* guilty.

দৌড়াদৌড়ী *s.* running to and fro.

দ্রব *ad.* melting, soft. দ্রব হঃ to melt.

দ্রব্য *s.* a thing, object.

দ্বয় *s.* a pair, couple, only used as the last member of a compound.

দ্বার *s.* a door.

দ্বাররক্ষক *s.* a doorkeeper, more commonly called দরবান *darwān.*

দ্বারা *prep.* by, by means of.

দ্বারী *s.* a doorkeeper.

ধ

ধন *s.* wealth. ধনক্ষয় expenditure of money.

ধনী *a.* a rich man.

ধর *v.* to seize, hold, carry.

ধর্ম্ম *s.* justice, religion; duty.

ধর্ম্মাবতার *s.* incarnation of justice, a term used in addressing officers of Government and persons in power.

ধারা *s.* method, conduct, usage; (in law) a section of an act or order.

ধার্ম্মিক *a.* religious, virtuous.

ধার্য্য *a.* which ought to be held, considered; suitable. ধার্য্য কর to impose (a tax, fine, etc.).

ধুতি *s.* a cloth worn round the waist, the sole clothing of the poorer classes.

ধুমধাম *s.* noise, uproar; pomp, display.

ধুঁআ *s.* (also written ধুয়া) smoke.

ধূর্ত্ত *a.* cunning, deceitful; *s.* a rogue, cheat.

ধুলি *s.* (also ধুলা) dust.

ধ্বংস *s.* destruction, ruin.

ন

নগদ *s.* (Ar. نقد) prompt payment, ready money, cash.

নতুবা *conj.* or, if not, otherwise.

নথী *s.* the file of papers composing the records of a case or lawsuit; the record.

নদী *s.* a river.

নব *a.* new.

নবনী *s.* butter.

নবনীত *s.* *id.*

নম্র *a.* humble, lowly.

নয় *v.* it is not.

না, নাই *ad.* no, not.

নাচ *s.* dance.

নাটমন্দির *s.* a theatre, dancing-hall in a temple.

নানা *a.* various, divers.

নাবালক *s.* (corrupted from Ar.-Pers. نابالغ) a minor, a young person below the age of legal majority.

নাম *s.* name.

নামঞ্জুর *a.* (Ar.-Pers. نامنظور) not approved, not sanctioned, rejected.

নামা *v. caus.* to bring down, pull down, let down; to cause to descend.

নালিশ *s.* (Pers. نالش) complaint; application.

নিঃসরণ *s.* issuing, uttering.

নিকট *ad.* near.

নিখুতি *s.* a kind of sweetmeat.

নিজ *pron.* own.

নিন্দা *s.* blame, reproach.

নিবেদন *s.* a respectful representation or request.

নিমিত্ত *s.* cause, reason; *ad.* for the sake of, in order to.

নিম্ন *a.* low, depressed.

নিম্নলিখিত hereinafter mentioned.

নিযুক্ত *a.* appointed, constituted.

নির্জন *a.* solitary, private,

নির্দিষ্ট *a.* fixed upon, determined, appropriated.

নির্বিরোধ *a.* unopposed, peaceable.

নির্মল *a.* pure, undefiled.

নিশ্বাস *s.* breathing, breath.

নিষ্পত্তি *s.* decision.

নীচে *ad.* below, down.

নীল *s.* indigo.

নীলকর *s.* an indigo-planter.

নীলাম *s.* an auction sale.

নূতন *a.* (corruptly written নোতন) new.

নোট *s.* (the English word) a note, bank-note.

ন্যায় *s.* justice; *ad.* resembling, after the fashion of.

প

পক্ষ *s.* a side, party. পক্ষে *ad.* on the side of, beside, in the possession of.

পঞ্চাইত *s.* (Hind. پنچایت) a committee of five persons, a village syndicate, sometimes corruptly written পঞ্চাৎ.

পটু *a.* clever, smart.

পড় *v.* 1. to fall, occur, happen; 2. to read, recite.

পণ্ডিত *s.* a learned man, sage.

পতি *s.* lord, husband. পতিপ্রাণা one whose husband is her life, a devoted wife.

পত্তনী *s.* a form of land tenure.

পত্তনীদার *s.* the holder of a *patnī* tenure.

পত্র *s.* a leaf, letter, document.

পথ *s.* a path, road.

পদ *s.* a foot, thing; rank; a sentence. This word is used as freely and vaguely as 'thing' in English, and its meaning depends a good deal on the context.

পবিত্র *a.* pure, clean.

পয়বস্তী *a.* erroneously written পয়বস্থি (Pers. پیوست) joined to, accreted to.

পয়সা *s.* a copper coin, one-fourth of an anna.

পর্ *a.* other. পর্নিন্দা blaming others.

পর্ম *a.* highest, chief, supreme.

পর্লোক *s.* the other world. পর্লোক যাইতে to die.

পর্শু *ad.* the day before yesterday, or the day after to-morrow, according to the context.

পরাক্রান্ত *a.* powerful, influential.

পরামর্শ *s.* advice; consultation.

পরিচয় *s.* introduction of one person to another, acquaintance.

পরিচর্য্যা *s.* service, attendance.

পরিত্যক্ত *a.* deserted.

পরিপাটি *s.* order, regularity.

পরিপূর্ণ *a.* filled, full.

পরিবর্ত্তন *s.* exchange, requital; alteration.

পরিবার্ *s.* wife and children, family.

পরিশ্রম *s.* toil, labour, fatigue.

পরিহাস *s.* laughter, joking, mockery.

পরীক্ষা *s.* examination, testing.

পরে *ad.* after, afterwards.

পর্গণা *s.* a division of a district, a county.

পরণাম *s.* (corrupted from প্রণাম) salutation, bowing.

পর্য্যন্ত *ad.* so far as, until, up to.

পশ্চাৎ *ad.* behind, after, subsequently.

পহর্ *s.* a watch, a period of three hours.

পহরা *s.* (Hind. پہرا) watch and ward; sentry duty.

পা *v.* to find, get, obtain.

পাঁচালি *s.* a particular mode of singing.

পাকশালা *s.* cooking-room, kitchen.

পাকা *v.* to cook, ripen; *a.* cooked, ripe, perfect, good.

পাচিকা *s.* a female cook.

পাঠ *s.* reading, a lesson.

পাঠা *v.* to send.

পাণ *s.* *pan*, the leaf of a vine (Piper betel) eaten with the areca-nut and spices.

পাপ *s.* sin, guilt.

পায়রা *s.* a pigeon.

পার্ *v.* to be able.

পার্শ্ব *s.* a side.

পালা *v.* (more correctly পলা) to fly away, escape.

পাশ *s.* a side; *ad.* near.

পিতল *s.* brass.

পিতা *s.* a father.

পিরাণ *s.* a shirt.

পিলা *s.* a child.

পিসী *s.* a father's sister, paternal aunt.

পিসীত *a.* descended from a paternal aunt, cousin.

পীড়া *s.* pain, trouble.

পীর *s.* (Pers. پیر) a Musulman saint.

পুত্র *s.* a son.

পুনর্বার *ad.* again, repeatedly.

পুরাতন *a.* old.

পুরী *s.* a city; a crowded set of apartments; one of the divisions of a large mansion.

পুরুষ *s.* a man.

পুষ্প *s.* a flower.

পুষ্পবৃক্ষ *s.* a flowering tree. পুষ্পপল্লব a flowering sprout.

পূজা *s.* divine worship, religious ceremonies.

পূজারী *s.* a worshipper; a priest who conducts the service, part of which consists in offerings of cooked rice; hence, a cook.

পূর্ *v.* to fill.

পূর্ব *a.* former, preceding, prior; east.

পূর্বক *ad.* preceded by, accompanied by; according to.

পূর্বস্থিত *a.* previous, placed first.

পূর্বে *ad.* formerly, before.

পৃথক *ad.* separate, apart from.

পেড়া *s.* edge, border.

পেশাকর *s.* (Pers. پیشه profession and کر doing) a prostitute.

পোড়া *a.* burnt. পোড়া কপাল (lit. burnt forehead) bad luck.

পোয়া *v.* to pass away, receive.

প্রকাশ *a.* clear, evident.

প্রকৃত *a.* real, true, genuine.

প্রজা *s.* people, subjects, generally used to express the cultivating class.

প্রতিপালন *s.* protection, maintaining and providing for any one.

প্রতিবাদী *s.* defendant, accused.

প্রতিবাসী *s.* neighbour. প্রতিবাসিনী female neighbour.

প্রথম *a.* first.

প্রথমতঃ *ad.* firstly, in the first place.

প্রধান *a.* chief, principal.

প্রফুল্ল *a.* expanded, blooming, gay.

প্রবৃত্তি *s.* effort, stimulus; inclination, tendency.

প্রবেশ *s.* entering, entrance; admission.

প্রভৃতি *ad.* et cetera.

প্রমাণ *s.* evidence, proof.

প্রয়োগ *s.* endeavour, exertion; authority.

প্রশংসা *s.* praise.

প্রশংসিত *a.* praised; (in polite language) mentioned.

প্রশস্ত *a.* wide, spacious.

প্রস্তাব *s.* proposal, mention.

প্রস্তার *s.* width, breadth.

প্রস্তুত *a.* ready.

প্রস্থান *s.* departure.

প্রাণ *s.* breath, life. প্রাণাধিক lord of life (husband). প্রাণ-ত্যাগ desertion of life (suicide).

প্রাতে *ad.* early, in the morning.

প্রায় *ad.* nearly, almost; just like; usually, generally.

প্রার্থনা *s.* prayer, entreaty.

প্রার্থিত *a.* prayed, entreated.

প্রিয়া *a.* dear (*fem.*); vocative *fem.* প্রিয়ে O dear one!

প্রেম *s.* love.

প্রেরণ *s.* sending.

ফ

ফজর *s.* (Ar. فجر dawn) morning.

ফটক *s.* gate, gateway.

ফয়তা *s.* (Ar. فاتحہ opening) the opening chapter of the Koran; prayers in general; offerings at the shrines of saints.

ফয়সল *s.* (Ar. فيصل) a decision.

ফল *s.* fruit; benefit, advantage.

ফসল *s.* (Ar. فصل cutting) crop, harvest.

ফাকী (also pronounced ফাঁকী) *s.* deceit, trick, imposture.

ফাট্ *v.* to break, crack, burst.

ফিট্‌ফাট্ *a.* very smartly dressed.

ফিতা *s.* tape, ribbon.

ফির *ad.* again; *v.* to turn.

ফুঁ *s.* blowing, puffing. ফুঁ দিতে to puff.

ব

বক্ *v.* to talk, chatter, babble.

বগলস *s.* (corruption of the English word in the plural) a buckle, buckles.

বজ্র *s.* thunderbolt.

বঞ্চিত *a.* tricked, cheated out of, deprived of.

বট *s.* a banyan tree (Ficus indica).

বড় *a.* great, big, large.

বৎসর *s.* a year.

বদনা *s.* a small water-pot with a spout, chiefly used by Musulmans.

বদলী *a.* exchanged, in exchange for; *s.* a substitute.

বধ্ *v.* to kill; *s.* killing, destruction.

বন *s.* a forest. **বনজাত** *a.* grown in a forest, wild (fruits, etc.). **বনভোজন** *s.* a picnic.

বন্দ *s.* an embankment; *a.* closed.

বন্দোবস্ত *s.* a settlement, arrangement, provision.

বন্ধু *s.* a friend.

বয়স *s.* age.

বরফী *s.* a sweetmeat.

বরাৎ *s.* an assignment of money, a warrant, cheque, order.

বরাবর *a.* even, level, equal; *ad.* equally, like to.

বর্খাস্ত *ad.* (corrupted from Pers. برخاست arisen, removed) dismissed from a post or appointment.

বর্ত্তমান *a.* present, existing; *ad.* at present.

বশ *s.* power, control. **বশ করিতে** to get under one's control, to manage, (vulgo) to twist round one's finger.

বস্ *v.* to dwell, sit.

বসতি *s.* a dwelling-house, habitation.

বহাদুর *s.* (Pers. بہادر brave) an epithet added to the name and titles of great men, meaning anything grand or bombastic the reader pleases.

বহু *a.* much, many; *ad.* very, exceedingly. **বহুবিধ** of many kinds. **বহুসঙ্খ্যক** *a.* numerous.

বা *conj.* or.

বাঁচ্ *v.* to survive, escape, live.

বাঁটোয়ারা *s.* (Hind. بٹوارہ) the partition of an estate between the several shareholders.

বাঁধ্ *v.* to bind, fasten, shut up.

বাক্স *s.* (the English word) box.

বাকী *a.* (Ar. باقی) remaining, the rest.

বাক্য *s.* a word, sentence.

বাগ *s.* (properly **বাঘ**) a tiger.

বাগান *s.* a garden.

বাচ্য *a.* expressible, describable.

বাজিআপ্তি *s.* (corrupted from Pers. بازيافت found again) a law term implying land resumed and assessed to land revenue.

বাটা *s.* a box for holding betel.

বাটী *s.* a house.

বাড়্ *v.* to grow, increase.

বাড়ী *s.* a house.

বাদী *s.* plaintiff, complainant.

বাদ্য *s.* music.

বাধ্ *v.* to hinder, prevent.

বাপ *s.* father, (a Hindustani word) used as an interjection of pain or surprise. বাপরে O father!

বাবৎ *ad.* (Ar. بابت) on account of.

বাবা *s.* an old man; (in nursery language) a child.

বাবু *s.* a respectable person, a title applied to all natives of respectable position, equivalent to 'Mr.'

বাবুআনা *a.* gentlemanly, like a gentleman.

বাম *a.* left (hand).

বারিবিহঙ্গ *s.* a waterfowl.

বারেণ্ডা *s.* a verandah.

বারওয়ারী *s.* a Hindu festival at which life-size figures made of clay and painted are exhibited.

বালক *s.* a boy.

বালিকা *s.* a girl.

বাসস্থান *s.* dwelling-place; residence.

বাসা *s.* a lodging, bird's nest.

বাহির *ad.* without, outside.

বিকট *a.* distorted, awry.

বিগলিত *a.* dropping, dripping, watering.

বিঘা *s.* a measure of land, usually about $\frac{1}{3}$ of an acre.

বিচার *s.* investigation, decision, judgment.

বিচিত্র *a.* variegated, various.

বিছানা *s.* bed-clothes, bedding, anything spread for sitting on.

বিজ্ঞ *a.* wise, learned.

বিদায় *s.* (Ar. بِداع farewell) dismissal, farewell, taking leave.

বিদিত *a.* known.

বিধবা *s.* a widow.

বিধা *s.* manner, form, rule. বিধায় in the capacity or quality of.

বিধাতা *s.* God, the Ruler of the world; Providence.

বিনামদার *s.* (Pers. بي نام دار) one who lends his name to another for transacting some business. Properly বেনামদার.

বিপদ্ *s.* calamity, misfortune.

বিবাহ *s.* marriage.

বিবেচনা *s.* discrimination, deciding; deliberating.

বিভাগ *s.* a share, division, portion.

বিরুদ্ধ *a.* opposed, hostile to.

বিলক্ষণ *a.* excellent, special, distinguished.

বিলম্ব *s.* delay.

বিলি *s.* division, allotment.

বিশাল *a.* large, vast, wide.

বিশিষ্ট *a.* excellent, select, special; provided with, possessing.

বিশেষ *s.* speciality; *ad.* especially.

বিষ *s.* poison.

বিষম *a.* irregular, evil, unmanageable.

বিষয় *s.* a thing, object; subject (of discussion).

বিহিত *a.* fit, proper, right.

বুজ্ *v.* to close (the eyes); to extinguish (a light).

বুঝ্ *v.* to understand.

বুটোদার *a.* flowered, embroidered with flowers or spots.

বুড়া *a.* old.

বুধবার *s.* Wednesday.

বৃক্ষ *s.* a tree.

বৃত্তান্ত *s.* circumstances, detail of particulars, information.

বেগ *s.* haste, speed, impetus.

বেটা *s.* a son, (contemptuously) a fellow.

বেড়া *v.* to walk.

বেলা *s.* time, the time of day or night.

বৈঠকখানা *s.* a reception-room, the outer room of a house in which visitors are received.

বৈরাগী *s.* a religious mendicant or devotee.

বোধ *s.* the understanding, intellect.

বোল্ *v.* (also written বল্) to speak.

ব্যক্তি *s.* a person, individual.

ব্যতীত *a.* past, gone, excepted; *ad.* except.

ব্যবহার্য *a.* used by, appropriated to.

ব্যয় *s.* expenditure.

ব্যয়ী *a.* expensive, lavish, extravagant.

ব্যস্ত *a.* distressed, agitated, annoyed.

ভ

ভগিনী *s.* a sister.

ভদ্র *a.* good, respectable. ভদ্র লোক the respectable people of a place, gentry.

ভদ্রাসন *s.* a well-to-do person's house and its surroundings.

ভয় *s.* fear.

ভর্ *v.* to fill; *a.* full, complete.

ভরা *a.* full.

ভাই *s.* a brother.

ভাগিনেয়ী *a.* a sister's daughter.

ভাঙ্ *v.* to break; *s.* hemp, used for smoking.

ভাত *s.* boiled rice.

ভাব্ *v.* to think, reflect, consider.

ভার *s.* burden, responsibility. ভারপ্রাপ্ত invested with powers, exercising the functions (of a post), authorized to act.

ভারী *a.* heavy, momentous, important.

ভার্য্যা *s.* a wife.

ভাল *a.* good.

ভিক্ষা *s.* alms, begging.

ভিজা *a.* wet, damp.

ভিতরে *ad.* within, inside.

ভিন্ন *a.* separate, distinct.

ভুক্ত *a.* eaten; comprised in, included in.

ভুড়ভুড়া *v.* to whisper, bubble up.

ভুঁই *s.* the earth; land, ground.

ভূভাগ *s.* a portion of land, a tract, area, field, plot.

ভূমি *s.* earth; land.

ভুরভুরা *a.* smelling of, reeking with.

ভৃত্য *s.* a servant. ভৃত্যবর্গ the servants (collectively).

ভেরী *s.* a trumpet.

ভোঁ *s.* sound imitating a loud noise.

ভোগ *s.* enjoyment, fruition.

ভোর *s.* early morning; dawn, daybreak (or even earlier).

ভ্রাতা *s.* brother.

ম

মঞ্জুর *a.* (Ar. منظور seen, looked at) approved, sanctioned.

মটর *s.* a pea, pease.

মণ্ডল *s.* a circle. মণ্ডলাকার circular.

মত *s.* a method, way; *ad.* like, in the same way as.

মতন *s.* a manner; *ad.* like, such as.

মত্ত *a.* drunken.

মদ *s.* spirits or any intoxicating liquor; drunkenness.

মধু *a.* sweet; *s.* honey. মধুপান drinking honey.

মধুকর *s.* a bee.

মধ্য *a.* middle. মধ্যস্থল *s.* centre, middle place. মধ্যস্থিত placed or standing in the middle or between.

মধ্যে *ad.* in the middle, between.

মন *s.* the mind.

মনান্তর *s.* difference of opinion, disagreement, quarrel.

মনোরঞ্জন *s.* delighting the mind, pleasure.

মনোহরা *a.* ravishing the heart, delicious.

মন্দ *a.* slow, bad, vile.

মমতা *s.* appropriation, attachment, affection.

মর্ *v.* to die.

মর্ম *s.* the heart, mind; the pith of a subject, meaning, point.

মর্মর *s.* marble.

মল *s.* dirt, filth; an anklet.

মহকুমা *s.* (Ar. محکمه) a court of justice.

মহল *s.* (Ar. محل place of alighting) a dwelling-place, palace.

মহল্লা *s.* (from preceding) a quarter or ward of a town.

মহা *a.* great, large (chiefly used in composition).

মহাজন *s.* (lit. great man) a money-lender.

মহাপাতক *s.* a great or heinous sin.

মহাপাপ *s. id.*

মহামহিম *a.* (lit. great greatness) one of the terms of exaggerated respect used in addressing a great man, meaning according to taste.

মহাল *s.* (plur. of মহল) an estate; a department of Government (in this sense it is nearly obsolete).

মহাশয় *s.* a gentleman, (as a title) Sir.

মহিমাসাগর *s.* Ocean of Greatness, title used in petitions etc.

মা *s.* mother.

মাচা or মাচান *s.* a platform, scaffolding, raised stage.

মাছ *s.* a fish.

মাতা *s.* (corruptly for মাথা q. v.); mother.

মাত্র *ad.* only, merely.

মাথা *s.* the head, top.

মান *s.* honour, reverence, esteem; rank.

মানব *s.* a man, human being.

মানস *s.* wish, desire.

মানুষ *s.* man, person.

মায়া *s.* illusion, delusion, deception; infatuation.

মার্ *v.* to kill, beat.

মারপীট *s.* (Hind. مارپیٹ) a beating, an assault.

মারফত *ad.* (Ar. معرفت) through, by means of.

মারফতদার *s.* an agent, intermediary.

মারুত *s.* the wind.

মাল *s.* wealth, property; goods and chattels.

মালিক *s.* (Ar. مالك) owner, proprietor (chiefly used of landholders).

মালিকী *a.* proprietary (rights).

মাস *s.* a month.

মাসী *s.* maternal aunt.

মাসীত *a.* descended from a maternal aunt, a cousin on the mother's side.

মিল্ *v.* to join; to agree with, meet; to be obtained.

মিলান *s.* comparison, reconciling, checking (accounts etc.).

মিষ্ট *a.* sweet.

মিসি *s.* a powder used to stain the teeth; sulphate of copper.

মুই *pron.* I.

মুকদ্দমা *s.* (Ar. مقدمه) a lawsuit, a case; an affair generally.

মুখ *s.* the mouth; the face. **মুখভঙ্গ** distorting the face, making a grimace.

মুড়া *s.* the end, top, or bottom of a cloth or other article; a border.

মুতালিকা *a.* (Ar. متعلقة) attached to, dependent on, connected with.

মুদ্ *v.* to fill up, shut (the eyes).

মূর্খ *s.* a fool.

মূল *s.* a root; the root of a matter. **মূলে** by reason of, by means of.

মূল্য *s.* price, cost, value.

মৃণ্ময় *a.* made of clay.

মৃত *a.* dead.

মেয়ে *s.* a woman; a female child.

মেরোয়া *a.* desperate, reckless.

মের্জাই *s.* (Pers. مرزاي princely!) a short jacket.

মোটা *a.* thick, fat.

মৌছুফ *a.* (corrupted from Ar. مَوصوف praised) the aforesaid.

মৌজে *s.* (Ar. موضع) a village (a term of revenue law).

ম্যাদ *s.* (corrupted from Ar. ميعاد) a period of time, usually the period allowed by law for certain acts. (More correctly **মীয়াদ**.)

য

যখন *ad.* when.

যথা *ad.* as, like as, for instance.

যদি *ad.* if. যদিও even if, although.

যা *v.* to go.

যাত্রা *s.* pilgrimage; play-acting, theatrical representation.

যিনি *pron.* whosoever.

যে *pron.* who, which.

যেন *ad.* wherefore, whereby.

যেমন *ad.* such as, like as.

যোগাযোগ *s.* machination, contrivance, connivance, collusion.

যোগ্য *a.* suitable; liable to, capable of.

র

রকম *s.* (Ar. رَقَم a mark) a number, numeral; a fractional share; a manner, method.

রক্ত *a.* red; *s.* blood. রক্তবর্ণ blood-coloured, crimson.

রঙ্গ *s.* paint, dye, colour.

রত্ন *s.* a jewel, anything valuable, a prize.

রন্ধন *s.* cooking. রন্ধনশালা cook-house.

রমণীয় *a.* delightful, beautiful, enjoyable.

রমজান *s.* (Ar. رمضان) the ninth month of the Mahommedan year, during which all good Musulmans fast in the daytime.

রাঁধ *v.* to cook.

রাক্ষস *s.* a demon, fiend.

রাখ *v.* to keep, preserve; to put, place.

রাগান্বিত *a.* enraged, angry.

রাত and রাত্রি *s.* night. রাত্রে *ad.* at night.

রাশি *s.* a heap; quantity.

রিপোর্ট *s.* (the English word) report.

রীতি *s.* custom, precedent, manner, method. রীতিমতে in due and customary manner.

রুমাল *s.* (Pers. رومال) a pocket-handkerchief.

রূপ *s.* form, beauty.

রূপা *s.* silver.

রুবকারী *s.* (Pers. روبكاري) an official proceeding, stating circumstances or facts and giving orders thereon.

রে *interj.* ho! hi! a contemptuous mode of address.

রেইল *s.* (the English word) rail; railings, railway.

রেশম *s.* (Pers. ريشم) silk.

রোহ্ *v.* to stop, hinder, obstruct.

রোদন *s.* weeping.

রোপিত *a.* planted.

ল

ল *v.* to take (inf. লওন).

লক্ষ্মীবন্ত *a.* fortunate, successful, prosperous.

লগ্ন *a.* adjacent to.

লম্বিত *a.* hanging down.

লা *s.* (rustic for না) a boat.

লাগ্ *v.* to stick to, be attached to, belong to; to touch, adhere.

লাঙ্গল *s.* a plough.

লিখ্ *v.* to write.

লুই *s.* a blanket, garment made of flannel.

লেখা *s.* writing.

লোক *s.* the world, a person, (pl.) people, folk.

লোচন *s.* the eye.

লোলা *s.* hanging loosely, swinging to and fro.

লোহা *s.* iron.

শ

শত *a.* a hundred.

শত্রু *s.* an enemy.

শব্দ *s.* a word.

শব্দিত *a.* echoing or resounding with words or noisy talk.

শলিতা *s.* the wick of a lamp.

শস্ত্র *s.* arms, weapons.

শাক *s.* a vegetable, herb.

শালা *s.* I. a brother-in-law, a common term of abuse; 2. (from Portuguese *sala*, a hall) a hall, large room, saloon.

শাস্তি *s.* discipline, punishment.

শাস্ত্র *s.* a book, the sacred writings of the Hindus.

শিখ্ *v.* to learn. শিখা *v.* to teach.

শিবরাত্রি *s.* the night of the 14th of Magh (dark half) sacred to Shiva.

শিরোধার্য *a.* placed on the head (in token of respect), obeyed.

শিরোনাম *s.* the heading of a letter.

শু *v.* to lie down to sleep.

শুদ্ধ *a.* pure, clean, upright. শুদ্ধচারিণী a virtuous, chaste woman.

শুন্ *v.* to hear.

শুভ *a.* auspicious, fortunate. শুভক্ষণ an auspicious moment.

শূন্য *a.* empty, free from.

শেষ *s.* the end; a remainder.

শোক *s.* grief, sorrow.

শোভা *s.* splendour, lustre, glory.

শ্রদ্ধা *s.* faith, belief; respect.

শ্রবণ *s.* hearing.

শ্রাবণ *s.* a month comprising half of July and half of August.

শ্রীযুক্ত *a.* illustrious, prosperous, fortunate; a title given to persons of respectable position.

শ্রীল *a.* much the same as the preceding; also used as a title.

ষ

ষোল *a.* sixteen.

স

সওয়া *s.* a quarter more than any number, e.g. সওয়া তিন three and a quarter.

সংবাদ *s.* news, information.

সংযমন *s.* restraint, control.

সংযমিত *a.* restrained, controlled.

সংশোধন *s.* purification, cleansing; rectifying, correcting.

সংসর্গ *s.* intimacy, association, familiarity, society.

সংসার *s.* the world, worldly state or condition.

সঙ *s.* a kind of singers.

সকল *a.* all, the whole.

সকালে *ad.* early in the morning.

সখি *s.* a friend.

সঙ্কল্প *s.* a ceremony; a contrivance; a thought.

সঙ্ক্রান্ত *a.* passed over; relating to.

সঙ্ক্ষুব্ধ *a.* agitated, tossed.

সঙ্গতি *s.* society; means, income.

সঙ্গী *s.* a companion, friend.

সঙ্গে *ad.* together with.

সজ্জন *s.* a good man.

সঞ্চার *s.* communication, contagion.

সতেজ *a.* vigorous; sharp, keen.

সদর *a.* (Ar. صدر) chief, principal.

সধবা *s.* a woman whose husband is living; opposed to বিধবা a widow.

সন্তান *s.* a son; offspring.

সন্তুষ্ট *a.* contented, satisfied.

সন্ধান *s.* search.

সময় *s.* time, season, opportunity.

সমর্পণ *s.* entrusting, making over to.

সমস্ত *a.* all, whole, entire, complete.

সমাকুল *a.* agitated.

সমাচার *s.* news, information.

সমুদয় *a.* all, complete; the whole.

সম্পত্তি *s.* wealth, property, prosperity.

সম্পদ *s. id.*

সম্পাদন *s.* producing, accomplishing, effecting.

সম্বরণ *s.* withdrawing, concealing.

সম্বোধন *s.* calling to, addressing.

সম্মত *a.* approved, consented to.

সম্মুখ *ad.* in front of; opposite to.

সরকার *s.* (Pers. سرکار) government.

সরাসরী *a.* summary, superficial.

সরীক *s.* (Ar. شریك) a partner, shareholder.

সরোবর *s.* a lake.

সর্ব *a.* all.

সর্বদা *ad.* always.

সর্বনাশ *s.* total destruction, utter ruin.

সলিল *s.* water.

সসপেণ্ড *s.* (the English word) suspend.

সহ্ *v.* to bear, endure, suffer.

সহোদর *s.* a brother.

সাকিন *s.* (Ar. ساکن) resident, inhabitant. (Often corruptly written **সাকিম.**)

সাক্ষাৎ *ad.* in presence of.

সাক্ষী *s.* a witness.

সাগর *s.* the sea, ocean.

সাজা *v.* to arrange, set in order; (euphemistically for) tutor a witness.

সাজা *s.* (Pers. سزا) punishment.

সাত *a.* seven.

সাথ *ad.* with, attended by, accompanied by.

সাদা *a.* (Pers. ساده) white.

সাধ্ *v.* to accomplish, effect.

সাধ্য *a.* possible, able, attainable: *s.* an object to be accomplished, power, ability.

সাবেক *a.* (Ar. سابق former) old, ancient, former.

সামগ্রী *s.* collection of goods.

সারস *s.* a crane.

সারি *s.* a row, range, line.

সার্থক *a.* efficacious.

সাল *s.* (Pers. سال) a year; used principally in writing dates.

সাহসে *ad.* boldly, rashly.

সাহেব *s.* (Ar. صاحب owner, lord) Master, a title applied to Englishmen in India.

সিংহ *s.* a lion.

সিঁধ *s.* a hole dug through a wall by burglars; a burglary.

সিকি *s.* a four-ana piece.

সিদ্ধি *s.* success; an intoxicating preparation of opium.

সিপাহী *s.* (Pers. سپاهی) a soldier.

সীমন্ত *s.* the parting down the middle of a woman's head. সীমন্তদেশ that part of the head where the hair is parted.

সুকুসুম *a.* having beautiful flowers.

সুখ *s.* happiness.

সুখী *a.* happy.

সুখ্যাতি *s.* good name, reputation, fame.

সুনির্মিত *a.* well built.

সুন্দরী *a.* a beautiful woman, a woman in general.

সুবাক্য *s.* kind speech.

সুবিধ *a.* easy, comfortable, suitable.

সুস্থির *a.* firm, composed (in mind), healthy (in body).

সূত্র *s.* a thread, series; an axiom. সূত্রে consequently.

সৃষ্ট *a.* created.

সে, সেই *pron.* he, she, it.

সেখানে *ad.* there.

সেবাইত *s.* worshipper.

সের *s.* a weight, about 2 lbs. avoirdupois.

সেলাই *s.* sewing.

সোণা *s.* gold.

সোপান *s.* a ladder, staircase. সোপানারোহণ ascending by a staircase.

সোবেরাত *s.* (corrupted from Pers. شب برات *Shab-i barāt* or night of offerings) a Mahommedan festival held on the 14th of Shaban.

সৌরভ *s.* fragrance.

স্তব্ধ *a.* made rigid, struck speechless with amazement.

স্ত্রী *s.* a woman.

স্থান *s.* a place.

স্থায়ী *a.* permanent, staying.

স্থির *a.* firm, steady.

স্নান *s.* bathing.

স্নেহ *s.* love, affection.

স্বত্ব *s.* 1. existence, being; 2. right, title, possession, property. স্বত্ববান *masc.* a rightful possessor. স্বত্ববতী *fem. id.*

স্বভাব *s.* nature, disposition, natural tendency.

স্বভাবজ *a.* self-grown, wild (trees or plants).

স্বর *s.* sound, voice.

স্বর্ণ *s.* gold.

স্বাদ *s.* taste, flavour.

স্বাধীন *a.* independent.

স্বামী *s.* lord, master; husband.

স্বার্থ *s.* one's own object. স্বার্থ-সাধন accomplishment of one's own object.

স্বীকার *s.* confession.

হ

হ *v.* to be (inf. হওন).

হংস *s.* a goose.

হজম *s.* (Ar. هضم digestion) digesting, (met.) embezzling.

হঠাৎ *ad.* suddenly, unexpectedly.

হর্ম্য *s.* a palace. হর্ম্যতল floor of a palace.

হাঁকাহাঁকি *s.* a calling and driving, hurrying, bustling.

হাঁড়ি *s.* a cooking-pot.

হাকিম *s.* (Ar. حاكم) a ruler, governor; judge, magistrate.

হাঙ্গামা *s.* (more correctly হঙ্গামা from Pers. هنگامه meeting) a hostile encounter, an affray.

হাট *s.* a weekly market.

হাত *s.* the hand.

হাল *s.* (Ar. حال) state, condition; *ad.* at present.

হাস্য *s.* laughter.

হিংসা *s.* harm, injury.

হিসাব *s.* (Ar. حساب) accounts, calculation, reckoning.

হুঁকা *s.* a pipe, a *hookah.*

হুকুম *s.* (Ar. حكم) order, command.

হুজুর *s.* (Ar. حضور presence) the presence of a great man, used as a respectful address to judges, magistrates, and other high officials, equivalent to 'your honour,' 'your worship,' etc.

হুড়াহুড়ি *s.* noise of a crowd, tumult.

হৃদয় *s.* the heart.

হেতু *s.* cause, reason.

হেতুবাদ *s.* a statement of reasons, preamble.

INDEX

N

THE END.